D0254729

OTHER WORKS BY EUGÈNE IONESCO

PUBLISHED BY GROVE PRESS

The Colonel's Photograph and Other Stories
Exit the King
Four Plays (The Bald Soprano; The Lesson; The Chairs;
Jack, or the Submission)
Fragments of a Journal
Hunger and Thirst and Other Plays (The Picture; Anger;
Salutations)
The Killer and Other Plays (Improvisation, or The Shepherd's
Chameleon; Maid to Marry)
Killing Game
Macbett
Notes and Counternotes: Writings on the Teacher
Present Past, Past Present: A Personal Memoir
Rhinoceros and Other Plays (The Leader;
The Future Is in Eggs)
A Stroll in the Air and Frenzy for Two or More
Three Plays (Amédée; The New Tenant; Victims of Duty)

A HELL OF
A MESS

A HELL OF A MESS

Translated by Helen Gary Bishop

Grove Press, Inc., New York

This translation copyright © 1975 by Grove Press, Inc.

All Rights Reserved

Originally published in French as *Ce Formidable Bordel!*, copyright © 1973 by Editions Gallimard, Paris.

No part of this book may be reproduced, for any reason, by any means, including any method of photographic reproduction, without the permission of the publisher.

ISBN: 0-394-17846-7
Grove Press ISBN: 0-8021-0071-6

Library of Congress Catalog Card Number: 74-29098

Caution: This play is fully protected, in whole or in part, or in any form under the copyright laws of the United States of America, the British Empire including the Dominion of Canada, and all other countries of the Copyright Union, and is subject to royalty. All rights, including professional, amateur, stock, motion picture, radio, television, recitation, and public reading are strictly reserved. All inquiries should be addressed to Samuel French, Inc., 25 W. 45th St., New York, N.Y. 10036.

First Evergreen Edition

First Printing

Manufactured in the United States of America

Distributed by Random House, Inc., New York.

GROVE PRESS, INC., 53 East 11th Street, New York, N.Y. 10003

CAST of Characters, in order of appearance:

Boss
Jacques Dupont
Pierre Ramboul
Lucienne
Character
Owner
Bookkeeper
Old Lady
Woman with the Dog
Husband of the Woman with the Dog
Man
Concierge

Cast of Characters

Old Man
Old Woman
First Man
Second Man
Waitress/Agnes
Proprietor
First Revolutionary
Second Revolutionary
Third Revolutionary
Woman Revolutionary
Woman
Mother
Young Man (her son)
First Policeman
Second Policeman
Another Man
Servant
Another Young Man
Mother of the Character
Character's School Teacher
Jacques Dupont's son
Agnes's Daughter
Son of the Lover of the Woman with the Dog
Son of the Revolutionary Who Punched the Character
in the Nose
Two Men
Another Woman

SCENE I

An Office.

The BOSS, JACQUES DUPONT, PIERRE RAMBOUL, LUCIENNE, *the* CHARACTER.

BOSS: It's not fair.

JACQUES: It's a dirty trick.

PIERRE: It's typical of him.

LUCIENNE: He inherited some money so he doesn't need to work. He's got the right to go.

PIERRE (*to* LUCIENNE): You always had a weak spot for him. Enough's enough!

LUCIENNE: Oh!

BOSS: When he needed us, we helped him. And now he's leaving, just like that. Clearing out. With three days' notice, take it or leave it. I should get the union on his back and have him fined. How am I going to find someone to replace him in three days!

PIERRE: It shouldn't be hard, he wasn't that good.

JACQUES: Don't I know it. He was a lazy slug. It's no great loss. I sat right across from him for fifteen years.

PIERRE: What's he going to do with his money?

BOSS: He could've invested it in my business.

PIERRE: With a guy like him it would only have caused you trouble.

JACQUES: I for one am delighted not to have to see his dumb face anymore. I was sick of him, day after day . . . day after day.

PIERRE: You were happy to go to lunch with him day after day though, and knock off a bottle of wine together. Every afternoon he'd fall asleep on his desk. You're the one who told me.

BOSS: I was a good egg. I let it go. I knew all about it.

PIERRE (*to* LUCIENNE): I'll bet you're feeling bad that he's going, eh?

LUCIENNE: I'd known him a long time.

PIERRE: In fact he was even your lover, right? A lover like him . . . Christ!

LUCIENNE: I chose you, didn't I? I left him for you, what more do you want?

PIERRE: He dressed like a slob.

BOSS: I was a good sport not to have kicked him out . . . on his ass. And now when he could give us some help with his money, nothing doing. No gratitude. He has a moral debt to us, the business needs capital.

JACQUES: I had political plans, ambitions. He's such a reactionary.

BOSS: There I disagree. No one could be further left than he is.

PIERRE: In any case his political feelings weren't worth a fig. In fact he never had any strong feelings about anything.

JACQUES: He used to tell me that nothing made any sense.

PIERRE: He's the one who didn't make any sense.

JACQUES (*to* PIERRE): And you think you make any sense?

PIERRE (*to* JACQUES): Look who's talking.

JACQUES: I still believe in . . .

PIERRE: Yes, we all know very well what you think you believe in. You tell us day in and day out, and it's always the same. It's a neurotic fixation.

BOSS: This is not the time to start arguing.

JACQUES: When he gets here, we'll tell him what we think of him.

PIERRE: Let's snub him.

BOSS: I'll do more than that, I'll give him a piece of my mind.

LUCIENNE: What has he done that's so awful? He has money now and he's going to do what he wants, that's all.

BOSS: You don't just drop people who've helped you. Besides, he's stupid. If he invested in the business, he'd make even more money. How can we make a profit when we've got debts?

JACQUES: Come on now, boss, you're just saying that so you can declare bankruptcy, but we know the kitty is full.

BOSS: Come look at the books, I've nothing to hide.

PIERRE: That's not Jacques' job, that's mine. I am the staff representative.

BOSS (*to* PIERRE): You had a lot of big ideas when you came to work for me. You came on like hot stuff. Where are all your ideas now? You've settled into a routine, not to say rut. You wore out fast, my friend.

PIERRE: We weren't talking about me but about him. I did what I could.

BOSS: What you "could" wasn't much.

JACQUES: I always thought he was a narrow-minded slob.

PIERRE: A narrow-minded bum.

BOSS: A bum is a slob who didn't make it.

JACQUES: When he'd come in in the morning, he wasn't even shaved. He stank of alcohol. If you think that was easy to sit across from, you're wrong.

LUCIENNE: He wasn't always like that.

PIERRE (*to* LUCIENNE): You're not going to say it's my fault because you left him for me.

LUCIENNE: I'm not blaming you. I never said anything like that. I wanted to leave him.

JACQUES: He said he was badly dressed because he didn't have enough money to buy himself a decent suit. You wait and see, he's probably bought the best suit in town to come to say goodbye. He wants to show us up.

LUCIENNE: He's not like that.

JACQUES: He stunk of boredom.

BOSS: That's because he didn't like to work. To work is to be happy. I am going to insist that he pay his moral debt to us. That should total at least $10,000.

JACQUES: The rat!

PIERRE: The fool!

JACQUES: To think there are still uncles left in foreign countries who don't know how to choose heirs.

BOSS: He kept his far-away uncle well hidden from us, I'll say that.

LUCIENNE: He didn't even know the man existed. He forgot about him long ago. He was his father's brother and he never even knew his own father.

BOSS: His mother killed herself for him. She begged me to hire him. She said he'd be grateful. Hah! Talk about gratitude.

PIERRE: A man like him doesn't know the meaning of the word. And to think of the way we all babied him.

JACQUES: He's not a real man.

BOSS: I should've fired him a long time ago; should've thought ahead. Sooner or later I would have thrown him out.

JACQUES: Too late to throw him out now.

PIERRE: You were too good to him, Boss.

BOSS: I like doing good. It's my weakness. No one will change me.

PIERRE: You're too good-hearted. You'll do it again.

BOSS: I'm too good-hearted. It's my nature. Someone will take advantage of me again.

JACQUES: The rat!

PIERRE: The fool!

BOSS: The ingrate!

BOOKKEEPER: He wasn't that bad.

LUCIENNE (*to the* BOOKKEEPER): That's what I say, he wasn't that bad.

PIERRE: He was a revolting human being.

The CHARACTER *enters stage right; his attitude and dress are modest.*

PIERRE (*toward him and at the same time to the others*): Ah, you're here at last my friend.

JACQUES: How nice of you to come and see your old pals.

BOSS (*shaking his hand*): You're very lucky. I congratulate you.

LUCIENNE: I'm happy to see you.

PIERRE: We're all happy to see you.

JACQUES: We're all happy for you.

PIERRE: And that's sincere, no jealousy at all.

BOSS: Now that you're rich, you're leaving us. We don't hold that against you. It's perfectly normal. No, no, believe me, you're absolutely right. Perhaps this type of work wasn't really for you. I would have liked to offer you a more important position. Unfortunately, in my modest organization there was no position worthy of you. I wanted to expand our operations, but we didn't have the capital to do it. I had plenty of ideas all right. You know we could've done big things, pulled some big deals together, you and I.

The CHARACTER *remains silent. They wait a moment for his reactions.*

JACQUES: I'd gotten used to you, old boy. All those years spent across from each other, almost all our young years. We were like brothers.

BOSS: For me, you were like a son.

PIERRE: And now, what are you going to do with your life?

The CHARACTER *remains silent.*

LUCIENNE: He doesn't know yet.

BOOKKEEPER: Let him think about it.

LUCIENNE: First he'll go away for a rest somewhere.

BOSS: Will you get married?

JACQUES: I hope he won't do anything as dumb as that!

PIERRE: For the time being he's going to take advantage of his money. He's still young, he can wait to see what happens.

BOSS: Aren't you worried about spending your capital? You'd do better to invest it . . . in something safe . . . at least a part of it.

Silence.

Oh, I don't want you to think I'm saying that so you'll put money into our business. However, you wouldn't be making a mistake if you did.

JACQUES: The Boss is only thinking of your own good.

PIERRE (*after a pause*): I put some money into the business too. I lost most of it though. The timing was bad.

BOSS (*to* PIERRE): Despite the bad timing, you got some of it back.

PIERRE: Yes, some. . . .

BOSS: But right now, a sizable investment (*winking at the* CHARACTER, *who remains silent*) . . . a sizable investment would make 10 percent. And a contribution would make 20 percent. We were in a recession. Now it's a flourishing market. I've got very solid associates.

LUCIENNE: Will you remember us? You won't forget us completely?

PIERRE (*to* LUCIENNE): That's why he's here, to tell us that he won't forget us . . . that he won't forget you . . . that he couldn't forget you.

BOSS: Of course, he's too sentimental for that.

JACQUES: Yes, that's right, he's sentimental.

BOSS: In any case, I want to thank you . . . yes, yes, I want to thank you for the help you've given us, for the time you were willing to work for us. Time is money, you know. But look here, it's almost lunch time. I'm buying everyone a drink at the Corner Café. Please, you can't refuse, it's only natural. You know that restaurant, the Corner Café?

JACQUES: We've spent many a happy hour there.

BOSS: Go ahead please, we'll follow you. (*To* LUCIENNE *and the* BOOKKEEPER.) Go on ahead please.

LUCIENNE *and the* BOOKKEEPER *follow the* CHARACTER *out.*

PIERRE: He's a rat.

JACQUES: I told you. He's a slob.

BOSS: An ungrateful pig. (*To* PIERRE *and* JACQUES.) After you, after you.

They all exit.

SCENE II

*A café-restaurant. The décor may be established instantly.
For example, the table from the previous scene in the office
can be placed differently. The lights are neon. The chairs
are rearranged. Behind the table which has become a
counter-bar, we see the* OWNER *of the café, who can be
played by the* BOSS *of the previous scene and who puts on
an apron, a mustache, and takes off his glasses, all in front
of the public. Bottles appear behind the bar, rows of them.
The* OWNER *could also be played by one of the other actors,
depending on the financial possibilities of the production.*
PIERRE, JACQUES, *the* BOOKKEEPER, LUCIENNE *and the*
CHARACTER *enter. The* BOOKKEEPER *is on the right, facing*

the counter. The others settle around the bar, empty glasses before them.

BOOKKEEPER: Would you like another round after this, sir?

JACQUES: Stay a little longer.

PIERRE: He trying to say he's got work to do. That's a laugh.

LUCIENNE: He's annoyed, I'll bet.

PIERRE (*to the* CHARACTER): He's annoyed because you're leaving already. You know, we get mad at each other, yell, sulk, but in the end we're all very fond of each other. You can't help it, working together for years the way we have.

JACQUES: It's been a whole life time. (*To the* CHARACTER.) Isn't that right?

PIERRE: Let's have another round. Then we'll go join the Boss.

JACQUES: We're in no rush, we don't have to be back before two o'clock. We've got to have one last lunch together to say goodbye. (*To the* CHARACTER.) No, don't jump for the check, this one's on me. When you come back to visit us, you can buy us champagne.

OWNER: This round is on me.

BOOKKEEPER: It's on me.

OWNER: The ladies are our guests, we're still old-fashioned around here. Cinzano all around?

PIERRE: That does the least harm.

JACQUES: Yeah, it doesn't put you to sleep, it wakes you up.

The OWNER *fills everyone's glass. They all empty their glasses bottoms up, at the same time.*

BOOKKEEPER: Now it's my turn.

JACQUES: We won't have you throwing company money around, dear lady. And as for your own, what would your husband say?

BOOKKEEPER: I'm single. (*Looking at the* CHARACTER.) We thought about getting married once. Now I'm single and I'm staying single.

PIERRE (*to* BOOKKEEPER): You didn't ruin your life because of him, did you?

BOOKKEEPER: I didn't say that. I've had one experience and that was enough, that's all.

JACQUES (*indicating the* CHARACTER): Our friend must feel bad to hear that.

BOOKKEEPER: I'll have to be going. I'm sure there are clients waiting.

She gets up and goes toward the CHARACTER, *who gets up also.*

I'll kiss you goodbye and good luck.

She kisses him. He sits down.

Will you come back to see us? Oh, I suppose you will.

She exits.

JACQUES (*to the* CHARACTER): You, with that shy look of yours, the way you dress and act—you still had the girls falling for you, eh?

PIERRE: The Don Juan of the Working Girl. Let's have another round. (*To the* CHARACTER, *who made a gesture saying it was on him.*) No, no, nothing doing. Later. This one is on me. (*To* LUCIENNE.) You'll miss him too, won't you?

They all knock back their drinks at once.

I've got to be going. (*To* LUCIENNE.) Say, why don't you stay for a while. I'm sure you'd like to say a private good-bye. (*With a hand slam on the* CHARACTER'S *back.*) You old roué, you, with your badly-shaved face and all. You get yourself a good suit, you hear! (*To* LUCIENNE *in a whisper.*) Don't go making a pass at him just because he's got money now. His money doesn't make him any less dirty or ugly. I know, I know, I didn't live up to the high hopes you had in me. It's still no reason to . . . (*Raising his voice.*) Okay, folks, I'm going. Have fun. Me, I have to go work, duty calls, ha, ha, ha.

PIERRE *exits.*

LUCIENNE (*to the* CHARACTER): Listen.

JACQUES: Let's have another round. Include yourself, Sam (*to* OWNER).

LUCIENNE (*to the* CHARACTER): Listen to me.

JACQUES (*to* LUCIENNE *and the* CHARACTER): If you two have things to say to each other, don't worry about me. I'm deaf and dumb when I have to be. Since everybody knows that there was once something . . . uh, between you. Well, damn it, what I mean is Pierre seemed to have such a great future in store for him when he came to work here . . . uh, when was it again?

CHARACTER: Five years and one month ago.

JACQUES: Five years and one month, that's uh, right. Well, he made a mistake putting money into the business, I'll tell you that. (*To the* CHARACTER.) You'll do well to keep yours for yourself. I'm with you. It's a lot smarter.

LUCIENNE (*to* CHARACTER): I left you a month later.

JACQUES: Hey, we can drink to your five years of wedded bliss.

LUCIENNE (*to* CHARACTER): Listen, listen to me please . . . I have to tell you . . .

She pulls him over to a small table where they sit down.

OWNER (*to the two of them*): I'll bring over your glasses.

JACQUES (*to the two of them*): Don't let me get in your way. I'll go drink with Sam at the bar. When it's over, I mean what you two have to say to each other, I'll come back and have a last farewell lunch, blood sausage with potatoes.

OWNER: It's the specialty of the house. You won't find better anywheres.

The OWNER *brings their glasses to* LUCIENNE *and the* CHARACTER. *He returns to the bar and says to* JACQUES, *who's there already.*

C'mon, one more, on me.

LUCIENNE: Look, since you're leaving no matter what . . . there's something I just have to tell you. Now I can tell you, before I couldn't. I acted stupidly with you. No, I'm not trying to get you back. But it wasn't all my fault, you know.

The CHARACTER *nods his head, agreeing.*

JACQUES: Did you see the headline in today's paper? What do you think? I wasn't surprised.

LUCIENNE: I didn't know what I was doing. And neither did you. I didn't understand what our relationship was about, where it was going. Now . . . now, I think . . .

OWNER: They want to wipe out small businesses, independent craftsmen. Something should be done.

LUCIENNE: I think we loved each other despite all the confusion. I know I loved you. But with you, you never know where you're at. You're so vague, so . . . undetermined . . . you should have expressed yourself . . .

JACQUES: Well just don't let them put anything over on you. We were talking about this problem just last night at the union meeting.

LUCIENNE: You didn't dare. You couldn't decide one way or the other. You really are a puzzle. With Pierre in the picture, yes, I know . . . you resent me because of Pierre. But I was so confused, I didn't know what to do, where to turn. When he arrived, he seemed so full of energy, will power, with a great career in store. He took me dancing, twice to the theater, to a swell restaurant where there was music. Soon afterwards however, he got bored with all the going out. That's when I understood

that I wasn't any worse off with you. He promised everything. That was his problem. You promised nothing.
That's your problem. But at least with him . . . for a
while at least . . . life seemed gay and worth living
. . . and then he lost his money. Under no circum-
stances should you even consider putting yours into the
business. It'll never be a successful enterprise. I have no
personal interest in saying that. I'm not saying it so that
you'll take me back. Besides, you've changed too. With
him everything looked rosy, with you everything looks
gray. Maybe it was my fault. I was so disappointed that
I couldn't make you get more interested in life, give you
more hope and enthusiasm. I just thought you didn't
love me enough. Maybe I was wrong. Maybe I was right.
If you had really loved me . . . well you know they say
that love can move mountains. Love bends iron, love
breaks through shackles. Nothing is stronger than love.
We all know that. At least, that's what they say. The
ones without guts give up on love. But real love never
gives up. Who knows, if things had been different, it
might have worked out for us. Perhaps a bright flame
was hidden under the ashes of our love. But all I could
make out then in the grayness of the ashes, was more
ashes. Perhaps it could have turned into a temple of love
once, with white columns and a shining altar . . . who
knows. Perhaps it was nothing but disorder and chaos.
Perhaps being so poor kept us from building more of a
life together, with the dull, dumb jobs we had to keep
working at. We could try again. It's not because you're
rich . . . yes, after all, maybe just because you are
rich, you'd be freer, you could help me be free. We could
travel, we'd see beautiful places, take planes, we'd go far,

over oceans, live on islands. Look, I have two gray hairs. And if the islands bored you, we'd . . . I feel so sorry for you. I feel that even now at this late date, I could still open the doors of the world for you, I could break your chains. . . . Can I have another drink? (*Calling to* OWNER.) Bring us another round, the same thing.

The OWNER *brings two glasses to them.*

OWNER: Here you are, kids.

JACQUES (*has been following the* OWNER *with his eyes and looks at* LUCIENNE *and the* CHARACTER, *who have fallen silent*): One more for me too. It's on him. Another drink is no burden to him.

The OWNER *returns to the bar, pours a drink for* JACQUES, *for himself.* LUCIENNE *and the* CHARACTER, *without speaking, drink their drinks slowly while the other two watch them.* JACQUES *and the* OWNER *knock their drinks down in one shot, look at each other, and wink.*

LUCIENNE: You really believe that it's all over? Do you? I shouldn't have told you what I did. I should have written you instead. One has time to think when one writes a letter. One expresses onself better. Oh, I know what you're thinking. You're thinking it's impossible, or that what I'm after is your money. Well, you're wrong. You've always been wrong. I suppose you'll go after a young girl now. With money you can get anything. And then again maybe you'll find nothing. Because you won't look for anything. Say something; I know you're listening to me. I know I'm not boring you. Well, I'm not so sure of that. In fact, I'm sure I am boring you. Oh, this is ridiculous. You'll be sorry, you know. Don't you remember once, it was spring, there were flowers. Do you at least remember the flowers? You'll be sorry, later on, you'll see. I'll be sorry too. You're so strange. Oh maybe you're not strange at all. I never could figure out what you were.

Silence.

I never figured out who you were, or what you wanted. You never talked much. But still every now and then you did say things. You would say that it was nice out, or that you loved me. Do you still love me? Do you still remember. . . . You can't pretend that nothing existed between us. I'd be sorry if you said it never meant anything to you. But it wouldn't be true even if you did. You would say that I had pretty legs and a beautiful body and lovely eyes. My legs are still pretty good. My eyes still shine. Listen to me . . . do you think there's any chance in hoping we could still . . . not right away . . . in a few days, a few months, I can wait. With Pierre, it was a disaster. I know, he's superficial. He talks through his hat. He's vain. He's more boring than boredom, much more boring than you. Will you come back and see me? Or write me, at least? Shall I give you the number of my postal box? Well, say something. Speak!

The CHARACTER *remains silent.*

Is that your last word? My hopes have been dashed twice. You're unhappy too. No, you're not even unhappy. Well, are you?

The CHARACTER *remains silent.*

I'm very sad, but I don't hold it against you. I guess I was wrong to think you were any different from the others.

Silence.

Okay, I'm going, or should I say, too bad but I'm going? A kiss goodbye . . .

She kisses him on the forehead.

Aren't you even going to kiss me "Goodbye" or "Till we meet again?"

The CHARACTER *stands up and kisses* LUCIENNE *lightly.*

CHARACTER: I . . . I . . .

LUCIENNE: Well, at least that's something. Write me. I know you'll write me. Oh, I don't suppose you will.

She drains her glass. Gets up. (To JACQUES *and the* OWNER.)

So long. (*To the* CHARACTER.) Goodbye and remember . . . I'll always be here.

She exits. The CHARACTER *sits down.*

SCENE III

The café-restaurant.

PIERRE, JACQUES, *the* BOOKKEEPER, *the* CHARACTER, *the*
OWNER.

JACQUES (*going over to the* CHARACTER's *table*): So that
dumb broad finally left, did she? I didn't want to disturb you, I knew you had so many things to say to each
other. I didn't want to listen in. I know how to be discreet. (*Yet he and the* OWNER *deliberately eavesdropped
during the whole scene.*) It's precisely because I know
the whole story that I can be discreet. (*Raising his glass*

high.) I brought my drink over to be with you. May I? You don't mind? Yes, there're no secrets around here. (*He sits down in* LUCIENNE's *chair.*) You mind if I sit down? Boy oh boy . . . fifteen years together, that's something. And that's why there're no secrets. That dumb broad! Oh, you're offended that I call her that . . . okay . . . Lucienne. Well Lucienne really stuck herself in it when she married that Pierre of hers. But you got there first with her anyway, eh? Oh don't think I was jealous . . . no, no . . . I had my girlfriend and then there was my wife, I was kept busy all right. You were right to take advantage of Lucienne. I don't want to hurt your feelings or anything, but I always wondered what she saw in you. You were always so washed-out looking, glumfaced . . . no glum is not the word . . . you were . . . sad looking, that's it. You always seemed to be coming back from a funeral. And I know you didn't even have a family. No friends either, not any you talked about anyway. You're a funny guy, but I liked you just the same. Didn't I say we were like two brothers? Let's have another, eh? Hey Sam, let's have another round. Include yourself too!

Moment of silence.

Well, what do you have to say? What do you plan to do with your loot? You're not going to pad the boss' pockets with it, I hope. He's given us the run-around long enough. He's a shark in sheep's clothing, that's what he is. A low-down shark, an enemy of the working class. We could have done things together, you know that? Started an independent labor organization within the company. With you, nothing works out. You don't give

a damn. You're so soft! You were afraid. It was too am-
bitious for you. You couldn't believe in it. Thirteen years,
no, fifteen, or was it thriteen? What was it, thirteen or
fifteen? How times flies. Life goes by, even when you're
doing nothing. But you never had any class conscious-
ness. Oh, I liked you well enough, I still like you,
you're like a brother . . . fifteen years together . . .
or was it thirteen . . . fifteen years, Jesus. Fifteen or
thirteen?

CHARACTER: Fourteen.

JACQUES: Sure, sure, fourteen, we'll cut it down the middle.
And what does a man do with his life when he hasn't
got something to believe in, an ideal? You've got to commit yourself to an ideal. (*To* OWNER.) Two more, Sam!

The OWNER *brings the drinks.*

Otherwise, you're bored, you're nothing, you're good for
nothing. One for you, and one for me. I tried to pull
you out of your funk, but nothing doing. You wouldn't
budge. All the wrongs of the world left you indifferent. I
really resented you for that. At the same time I had a soft
spot for you. We were like brothers after all. Fifteen
years together, across from each other. Or was it thirteen?

CHARACTER: Fourteen.

JACQUES: You have no idea how much people like you are
responsible for the current state of society. (*He points his
finger accusingly.*) YOU are responsible. All the rotten
tricks that the establishment gets away with while working within the system, you have to answer for. Your in-
difference underwrites it, covers it, justifies it. If you

want to know what I think . . . the real culprit is you. It's all the fault of people like you. Yeah I know, how can I talk like this after all the years we spent together, fifteen or thirteen, no difference. But how do you expect us to change the system if guys like you don't help? However, with the money you've got now you could really do something, make up for lost time. You could help us. No point giving money to the poor. They've got to wallow in their misery until they're ready to revolt. The money should go to the worker's unions. We're the ones who pay the thinkers, the journalists, the militants, the workers. But I don't suppose you understand any of that. You're too selfish. Hey, Sam, let's have another pair here. Only my friend isn't drinking any more. Pour two anyway, one'll be for you. (*Back to the* CHARACTER.) If I asked you to make a contribution to help me organize a strike, you'd think I was going to blow it on booze, eh? Well, forget it. I don't want your dirty money. You're a prick!

OWNER (*bringing* JACQUES' *drink and knocking his own back in one shot*): Hey, you shouldn't say that to him, Jacques. We're all pricks sooner or later.

JACQUES (*knocking his drink back too*): Some more than others. However, the rest of us are victims of objective conditions.

OWNER: Well, you know something, I've worked all my life. I never even got my high-school diploma. . . . I went from a sweeper in a hair-dressing parlor to a waiter in a restaurant. . . . Working like a dog the whole time, I finally earned enough to buy my own four walls, my restaurant, where I'm the boss. Well I'll tell you, my money, well I'm gonna hang on to it. I'm not gonna go giving it to anybody who asks. Let the others sweat a little too. If I made mine, they can make theirs, that's the way the system works.

JACQUES: That's the jungle, dog eat dog. You're a capitalist. You're an enemy of the people.

OWNER (*to* JACQUES): And you, you're a dreamer who's a loser, that's what you are. If you don't get something out of life, you may as well hang yourself. Well me, I'm gonna get something out of it. Just watch me.

JACQUES: Great, what do you get out of it, I'd like to know. You work from morning to night, from dawn to midnight. You're alienated like all the others.

OWNER: That's not true. I have fun too. I drink with my clients and my clients are my buddies. (*To the* CHARACTER.) Isn't that right? I've treated you well, haven't I? For how long now, fifteen years or thirteen that you've been eating in my place, every single working day?

JACQUES (*to the* CHARACTER): I like you anyway. (*To the* OWNER.) I like you too. Bring three more drinks and we'll toast. This is a democracy after all. (*To the* CHARACTER.) Don't mind me, I'm just a little bit nervous that's all. I'm going to have to get used to your not being around. Get used to somebody else. I loved you like a brother. You always had a cold and you were always blowing your nose and snivelling into dirty handkerchiefs. I got used to it. I'll have to get used to the dirty handkerchiefs of the new guy. He'll be okay I suppose,

but he won't be you. He'll have his own habits like cleaning out his ears or something like that, or picking his
nose, or spitting on the floor. He won't be a member of
the New Society, that's for sure. (*To the* OWNER, *pointing to the* CHARACTER.) He wants another drink. Bring
three more. Oh, I don't give a shit about the Boss, we
don't celebrate every day and since we're celebrating
your departure for bigger and better things . . . I think
I'd like to celebrate the departure of the new guy already.
If I have to wait another fifteen years for him to leave,
I'll be retired by then. Hah, once I retire, then I'll have
lots of time to organize some changes in society. You'll
see, things will change. In the meantime, can we have
something to eat? It's on him. Beef stew for the two of
us . . . for the three of us. And some wine, and not any
of that table wine either, some good stuff from the cellar.
Something subtle . . . Beaujolais!!

OWNER: I can do better than that . . . I've got a Burgundy that's real special. Furthermore, it goes better with
the stew; boeuf bourguignon with Burgundy, get it? Ha,
ha, you see there's always something to laugh at in life,
you just have to look for it.

JACQUES: You're so right. . . . Just bring us the bottle
and leave it.

OWNER: I'll bring the beef too while I'm at it. Don't go
away, ha ha.

JACQUES: Now where was I? Oh yes, I wanted to say that
the only way to get any justice in this world . . . is to
organize, that's right.

The OWNER *comes with the food.*

Here, sit right down with us, Sam. Take a chair. (*He does.*) Now, I was saying about justice. . . .

OWNER: Oh, I forgot the wine!

JACQUES: The one element that's most important . . . in fact, absolutely essential, and you'll see that I'm right on this . . .

The OWNER *returns with the bottle and the glasses. He pours the wine and the three of them touch glasses in a toast.*

Here's to you.

OWNER: To you.

JACQUES: Here's to my pal . . . fifteen years working together, you know, that counts . . . how am I going to manage with the new guy? Here's to you and to you. Fifteen years together, or thirteen, no difference, it counts in the life of one man. You can say what you want, but it's nothing to sneeze at. Here's to the both of you . . . because like I was saying, and you better believe me . . . hey, the bottle's empty.

OWNER: I'll bring another.

JACQUES: Hold on, we'd better take it easy.

OWNER: Three more glasses, it's on me.

The OWNER *brings the glasses to the bar, fills them quickly, and returns.*

JACQUES: Well, the Boss can squawk if he wants to, but I'm not going back to the office today. It's special today 'cause it's the last time we're seeing each other. Oh I know it's not really the last 'cause you'll come back to see us . . .

OWNER (*to the* CHARACTER): I always took good care of you, sir, you've got to admit that. You'll come back to see us I'm sure. You'll never get better service than you've had in my place.

JACQUES: To you.

OWNER: To you.

They drink their wine bottoms up. The OWNER *runs to fill their glasses faster and faster in what becomes a steady, uninterrupted manner.*

JACQUES: You'll come back, friend . . . a man doesn't forget his pals. Oh I know we had our tiffs . . . I used to pick on you at times, I'll admit that . . . oh well, it's up to you to decide. Deep down though, I'm sure you'll convert. Hah, not to go to mass, no! You'll convert to the movement, sooner or later.

The OWNER *and* JACQUES *touch glasses.*

Here's to you, and to you. Now it's my turn.

CHARACTER: No, it's mine.

The OWNER *runs to fill the glasses and returns.*

JACQUES: Thirteen years together, no, fifteen.

OWNER (*still busy bringing back filled glasses from the bar*): You'll never have a better boeuf bourgignon, sir . . . it's my specialty and I'll brag about it. And there's nothing wrong with my red bean stew either.

JACQUES: For all we know, you've already been replaced. Hah, I'd like to see what the other guy looks like, I got so tired of looking at you after fifteen years . . . boy oh boy. Here's to you.

OWNER: Here's to you. Yeah, there isn't another red bean stew like mine in all of Paris. My mother was from the South where there was no cider. She taught me to make it with real wine. (*He runs to get more wine.*) Some make it with beer, not me! Beer's for the Krauts!

JACQUES (*to the* CHARACTER): I didn't say that to be mean.

OWNER: The war, you remember? The Krauts were tough but they were fair. A soldier's a soldier, we were all the same.

JACQUES *and the* OWNER *touch glasses with the* CHARACTER.

Here's to you, friend. I can call you a friend, can't I? After all, you've been eating in my place for fifteen years now.

JACQUES: Fifteen years, working together, day after day after day. It's a good thing there were the nights, ha, ha.

OWNER (*bringing more wine*): You really lived it up at night, you rascal. (*Pointing to the* CHARACTER.) Not him!

JACQUES: Hah, you don't know him. He had his Lucienne. He had his Janine, too. Yeah, that's right, you wouldn't think so to look at him would you?

THREE TOGETHER: Here's to you.

Continued coming and going of the OWNER.

JACQUES: Fifteen years at the same job. I don't give a shit about the Boss! And you, I was sick and tired of your face. But we're friends anyway, right?

THREE TOGETHER (*with fresh wine in their hands*): Here's to you.

JACQUES *and the* OWNER *embrace. They each embrace the* CHARACTER, *who tries to dodge their drunken affection but finally allows himself to be embraced.*

SCENE IV

The CHARACTER'S *unfurnished apartment.*

The CHARACTER; *an* OLD LADY.

The stage is empty. There is only a chair, stage front left. Standing in front of the seated OLD LADY *is the* CHARACTER *dressed as in the preceding scenes: gray coat, gray hat, black shoes. When he takes off his coat, he will naturally be wearing a gray suit. He wears a black tie.*

OLD LADY (*middle class, wearing a hat with a great hat pin showing, a dark suit, of course*): Now don't you worry one bit, you'll have no trouble at all furnishing your

apartment. Do as I did, buy the whole thing at Sears.
They have a store a few blocks from here. You can always depend on their quality and their home decorating
service is excellent. And what they don't have here, they
order at once from their warehouse. Just because we're
in the suburbs, don't think we want for anything. Not
one bit; this is a very commercialized suburb and we have
everything and then some. Well, now that you've bought
this apartment, I can tell you you've done the right
thing. With all the construction going on these days,
they all try to sell you apartments by showing you the
floor plans. I don't know if you're like me, young man,
but I don't understand anything about floor plans. Besides, all this modern construction is just thrown together, just another way for promotors to make more
money. Their buildings never last more than twenty
years; that way they can build new ones. It's much better to see what you're buying; what you see is what you
get. Floor plans can be deceiving. In new buildings the
walls are paper thin; you can hear your neighbors
sneeze, you can hear the toilet flush, you can hear what
they say, if they spit, everything. I won't say any more,
you get the picture. Real estate is the best investment,
we all know that, and that's what I've always done, but
in good real estate, good solid buildings, not stuff made
out of hollow bricks and compressed paper. Young man,
I've tried everything, and believe me, it's still real estate
that pays the best. With investors you always get taken.
You give them your money, they promise 8 percent, 9
percent, 10 percent, 11 percent, 12 percent and before
you know it, they've absconded with the funds. They're
all thieves. You'll say, who is not a thief these days? I

know there are people who say it was always like this, but I don't think so. Things used to be more honest. There were still people who believed in living from their hard work, who took pride in their work. Now no one cares anymore. Naturally you'll have to invest some of your money, with precaution, so that it will earn you an income and not use up your capital. I would choose an agricultural-cooperative type of bank myself, but I certainly don't want to influence you. For me agricultural banks inspire the most confidence because they are built on wheat. Nothing is more solid than wheat, young man. Without it, there's no bread, no spaghetti, the staples of life. Stocks and bonds are just so much paper, and during these times of economical crisis, they mean nothing. Well here you'll be comfortable and content, I'm sure. The building is neither old nor new, you're on the third floor, you're on the outskirts of town, the heart of the city is not far away, if you feel like going there; you have subways, buses, and, if you're in a hurry, there are taxis of course. This house is almost a hundred years old, you know. But you won't be needing to go to town often, you're retired after all. Oh, the entrance to the apartment is a bit dark, I know.

The CHARACTER *follows the gestures of the* OLD LADY *as she details the aspects of the apartments.*

But then nobody spends time in the entrance, you just pass through quickly. It's to go in and go out, that's why it's called entrance. Near the door, there, on the left, is the toilet, as you no doubt noticed. It's good plumbing, let me tell you, had it put in myself. When you pull the chain, it won't remain in your hand. You're looking at

the walls. Naturally a coat of paint would make them
look better. And then you have the glass door there
which gives onto the parlor where we're standing. As you
can see, there is light from three windows. It's big, airy,
just right for a sitting-dining room. And alongside the
toilet is the kitchen, and then facing the courtyard there
are the two bedrooms. One of them can be your bedroom
and the other, well who knows, you're still young enough
to maybe need a room for a little baby one day. It's much
better for a man to grow old with a companion. Being
alone is not always fun. But I don't mean to butt into
your business, I don't want to influence you. It's just
my opinion, it doesn't have to be yours. When you have
children, you have problems too, there's always that to
look at. They can be ungrateful, not always, but often;
there're good ones and bad ones. Anyway you have to
look at the good side of life, eh? If you don't get married,
well you can always turn the extra room into a store-
room . . . for your luggage, your off-season wardrobe.
In this room here, as you can see (*she points in the
direction of the audience*), there is this window which
looks out over a side street, and to the left (*he looks*) the
other window which looks out on the main street at the
end of the block. There are trucks and buses, and a
little bit of noise, I can't deny it, but it's not directly under your windows at least. For me it was a kind of background sound, it relaxed me, put me to sleep. Well,
everyone is not like me of course, some people are
bothered by it. I do hope you, however, are like me. And
from that other window there is the side street, as I said.
It's a whole other show from there, it's the small town
atmosphere entirely. On one side, you have the big city,

and on the other, the small town. It's very quiet and peaceful on this side, young man. With a few steps, you're miles away from the din. It's as quiet as anything, as a cemetery. But a live cemetery, let me say that. Nothing but old retired folks, not young retireds, like you, but old ones. There's the White Russian, a very well educated gentleman. He's a duke, a real duke, fled Russia during the revolution. Can you imagine, chasing people like him, so polite and elegant and everything? He's always walking his dog, a lovely little doggy, as polite as his master. Like master, like slave, as they say. The lady on the second floor has a poodle too. He, however, is not well behaved. And his mistress is no better. He once bit my shoe. On this little street you can see cottages with front yards and courtyards and trees; and there, right across, there are two old people, so old, and they're just like a pair of lovers. They go out together, shop together, supporting each other, it's so sweet. They're always together on their little canes, they kiss, it's charming. Each time I see them they bring tears to my eyes. And to the right of their house there's that other little house you see, an old man lives alone in there, you'll be seeing him. He goes out every day except when he's sick. He's not a very happy one, that one. That's why I said to you it's better to be married. I warn you, young man, don't end up like him. And to the left of the little house, you see where that fat nanny is, well that's not a very happy scene either. She sits out there every evening, in front of her door, waiting for her son, and that's been going on for twenty years now. He left for war or for some foreign country, we don't know and neither does she, it's so long ago. She still believes he'll come back. We don't! But she's there every night, sitting in her chair, with an umbrella when it rains, waiting, waiting. . . . She never speaks. Only a few years ago, she still talked about it, she cried, she complained, she ran in with tears streaming down her face. Now she's a lot calmer. She doesn't talk to herself anymore. She stays there until nightfall, then she takes her chair and goes inside. But with these little exceptions, young man, it's a very happy little neighborhood. In the springtime, there are flowers in all the gardens, big ones, small ones, and the big ones are really big, not like the kind you find in the city window boxes. And in all colors. They grow much better here than they do in the city and much better than in the northern suburbs. Here in the southern suburb it's warmer naturally. And every Sunday, especially on Sundays, the sky is so blue. It starts getting blue on Thursdays usually. And since we're so much closer to the equator than the northern side of town, the sun is bigger and closer. The days are longer and the nights are full of stars. Sometimes I used to watch them when I had insomnia or when I'd get back from the movies. It was with my husband that I used to go to the movies. He's dead now and that's why I sold you the apartment. I can't live here without him, but I'll miss my friends from the little street down there. I can't stand it here alone anymore. Oh, if you had only known him, young man. You can't imagine what it's like to be a widow. Oh, I don't wish that on you at all. We were never separated. For forty years. He knew every trade there was. Shopkeeper, businessman, contractor, theater technician, machinist; he even had a laundromat which is not far from here; he left that to his partner. Say, you could take your laundry there, now that I think of it. He was also a station master for the railroad once. He wanted to become a policeman and he had talent for it too. Oh he was so well read, he had read every murder mystery ever written and he had a wonderful collection of them too. He was handy around the house too. Well, a good example of that is the toilet, it wasn't the plumber who finally put it right, oh no, it was him. It's never broken since. He died just like that, in one second. We were here talking one evening, he had a difficult day that day. He had had trouble with a merchant and he was a little upset by that, and then we had a few words, nothing serious. He'd always pick little fights with me when he had trouble with a merchant. But we made up in front of the fireplace right there, next to the chimney where there were two armchairs facing each other. I was doing my crocheting and he was reading his mystery or the crime page of the newspaper, I don't remember. He was a good man despite his interest in crime, believe me. He was just satisfying his imagination maybe, I don't know. And then he put his hand on his heart, he got up, and that frightened me, so I said: "Jean, what's the matter?" He fell his full length to the floor, young man, his full length and he was tall, over six feet. When I saw him lying there on the floor like that, he looked like twelve feet, like a column which had just fallen. I called the doctor, I called the priest, I was hysterical. I never thought it could happen. I never even thought about it at all. I stupidly believed that we'd be here forever. I cried in the priest's arms. He said I should have expected it, it happens to all of us. Sooner or later, but it happens. The good Lord called him, he said. Well, Jean

never believed in the good Lord. I did, I'm religious, I
know one day I'll find him waiting under a tree in some
flower garden. The doctor told me he died of heart ar-
rest. I asked him, "How does a heart get arrested?" and
he said, "It just stops and we die." And he was so strong,
like a bull. He could have squashed you with one hand.
We got along well. Once, I remember, he was drunk,
he slapped me, my nose started to bleed, he had broken a
tooth, but he was so sorry, he apologized. Oh, he was
a sophisticated man. I can't live in this house without
him. I'm going to live with a single niece who lives in
a little seaside town in the South. She has two rooms
and it'll be enough for the two of us. My niece wants to
retire, so with her pension money and the money I'll
contribute from the apartment, and a few bonds, we can
live very modestly but well, the two of us. Our needs are
not great but at least we'll live without worries for however long we last, ten years or fifteen, maybe twenty, who
knows. Now that I've seen death, I know that I'm going
to die, that everything has an end. When I think that
death didn't exist for me! Well, that's why I'm going to
live with my niece; I don't want to die all alone. I won't
be a burden on her, since I'm bringing my own money
and paying my own way. I wouldn't want to be a burden on anybody, because I know one thing, young man,
anyone who's no longer worth anything but who needs
care and attention, well everybody wants them dead as
soon as possible so as to be rid of them. For example,
I myself had to take care of my grandmother because
my mother died young. Well, when granny died I
breathed a sigh of relief. Not that I didn't love her, I
did, you have no idea how much I loved her. Once she

was gone, I got married. So now you have to prepare for everything. I'm old. My niece isn't young any more. So we started to think ahead, prepare. I've thought about her future too, once I'm gone. With the money she gets from selling our little apartment, she'll find a place for herself in an old age home of good quality, yes, good quality, because that's important. I've seen some rotten ones, let me tell you. But when old people are in a good home, and well taken care of, they go without even being aware of it. They lose weight and get thinner and thinner, they walk around the grounds with their canes, getting thinner and thinner so that soon you hardly see their shadows, not telling the men from the women. You think they're still there 'cause you see their shadows, but soon you don't even see those, they disappear slowly like a filmy cloud in front of the sun. In the other homes, the bad ones, they're badly treated, young man, I know that for a fact. They even deliberately kill them, I've been told, with injections, just because they're too much trouble to care for and there are too many of them. They have no money, so they're exterminated. Ah yes, if the truth were known, but these things I know for a fact. Well, young man, you furnish this apartment according to your own taste . . . (*she gets up*) I wouldn't want to influence you and to prove it, I'll be on my way.

CHARACTER: Tell me, madame, is there a café-bar in the neighborhood?

OLD LADY: Certainly there is, young man, I told you we had everything. Right down there at the corner of the street. They have everything you could want. I used to go there sometimes with my husband and we'd come back a little tipsy, the two of us. (*With* savoir vivre.) They have an excellent selection of spirits, the finest wine cellar, a great variety to satisfy the most sensitive tastes. . . . I must be off to prepare for my trip, young man, allow me to take my leave. (*She goes to the door, she turns around to say*) I almost forgot, just between us, be careful of the concierge.

She exits.

SCENE V

The CHARACTER'S *apartment.*

The CHARACTER; *the* WOMAN WITH THE DOG.

The WOMAN WITH THE LITTLE DOG *enters from the front door.*

WOMAN WITH DOG: How do you do, sir? I'm not disturbing, am I? Well, I couldn't be, since there's nothing to disturb here, is there? Oh, there's a chair, may I sit down? I live just downstairs, door to the right on the second floor. I noticed you when you came to see the apartment the first time. You did right to buy it, it's a good investment in real estate. The old lady who sold it to you is nice enough. She must have told you that she's a widow, right? She told you about her husband, eh? She always tells her tale to everyone. She's a talker, rambles on and on, it must be age. I'm not like that at all. Aside from that, she's very nice. We'll miss her. You know I love to get to know the other people in the house. Do you play bridge? I like to have little gatherings, of the people in the house, I mean. It makes things more chummy. No one should live like a hermit. Besides, one always gets bored by oneself, right? I was told that you're retired and you don't want to work anymore, that you inherited money. You see, we know everything already. There isn't much that doesn't get known, is there? Not that I asked questions, mind you. I was told, that's all, by the concierge, as a matter of fact. She tells everything, watch out for her. It's not that she's mean, she's just a blabbermouth, so without meaning to she says bad things about people, but she's not really malicious. You know how concierges are . . . tongues like vipers. It's professional deformation, that's what it is. But it's the mouth one has to worry about, nothing else. Actually, she's very helpful with errands and housework and things. You just have to give her a little tip every now and then. Oh not very much, we don't want to spoil her. Now, we've got to get you married soon, don't we? Or will you get married all by yourself? One should be married. Only me, I suffer sometimes. I didn't always live in the suburbs, you know. That's why I'm such a social person; however, the little get-togethers I spoke of are not formal at all. They're much more family affairs. The tenants of the house, a few neighbors, it's like a family, right? But don't think that I invite everyone. You, for instance, I'd invite right away. One can see that you're a gentleman, a man of the world. Isn't my dog sweet? I had seven, you know. What a job that was. They need taking care of just like children. It was because I didn't have any children. It's not that I didn't want any. It's my husband's fault. I'll leave it at that, I won't go into any details. He's a very stubborn man, my husband, and marriage is sometimes hell, let me tell you. He's not like me at all. I'm always doing things for him, full of little attentions. Can you imagine, seven little dogs and my husband! I was a veritable slave. They're cute, but you're still a slave. He's sweet too, but he's always complaining, needing things, hand me this, get me that. It was his idea to come live in the suburbs. He didn't want to see anyone anymore. Don't be like him, friend. He's sorry now, but it's too late. Sometimes we think about moving, but apartments have become so expensive in the city. My husband has stocks and we've got money saved, but these days, what with inflation and all, what you're worth is worthless. Well, worth *less*, at least. While everything else goes down, the cost of living keeps going up. That which should be going up comes down, and that which should be coming down goes up. There are times when I think I can't take it anymore. Always the same apartment, the same gossip, the same problems, I'm fed up. Oh, I've tried to run away, but I always come back. I can't leave the house all alone and my husband being so nervous and all, someone's got to watch over things. You don't believe me. I look happy-go-lucky, I'm still young, I'm not homely, that's what they tell me, at least; that's right, men turn around in the street to look at me, but I never pay attention. When I think of him sitting there with nothing to do but fret and complain. He has everything he wants and he's always bitching. He has no patience, he's too nervous, and he doesn't know how to look at the good side of life. If you don't look at the good side of life, what's left for us? We couldn't go on living. But can we go on living as it is? We want to live for life but we don't, we just fritter it away. We're always making mistakes, going wrong. Well, anyway, as I was saying, I always come back in the end. I come home tired. But still I'm happy to find my old man and I get started right away, organizing my get-togethers. And soon it becomes routine and monotonous again. The enthusiasm never lasts long. And then I can't stand it again. I suffocate, yes, literally suffocate. And then I take off again. And I come back. And I leave. And I come back. That's how it's always been. Where can one go, I ask you? And where can one stay? I want everything and I have nothing, or maybe it's that what I have seems like nothing to me. Oh, if only I could begin again. I'd know how to do things right if I could do them again. You bet I'd do it right. I'd make other mistakes, of course. Life is dumb, eh? Oh, there are others who are a lot worse off, so there's no point in taking things so seriously. It's just the boredom that's killing, the boredom. Now I'm a little crazy, a little, not too much, one can't go overboard even in craziness. Now, do we live for nothing? They say not. They say there's meaning to life. But who knows for sure? The one who's got the answer to that one is very clever. But that is the question. We should always be able to see beyond our own lives to something else, some higher ideal. We should never be looking lower. We should remain aware that there are others who are more miserable than we, instead of being obsessed with those who are more happy. So we console ourselves with the thought that things could be worse, but, I ask you, is it reasonable to expect us to be satisfied with being less worse. Can I really be happy with being less worse? Ah, this stupid world is no fun. Forgive me for speaking so frankly. I hardly know you but you inspire confidence. And besides I have a very direct, sincere nature. I like speaking frankly. I say everything I'm thinking, even to my husband. Well he, for one, doesn't like that. He doesn't like me to say what I've got on my mind. That's the way it is. What more can people expect from a person after all? What do they want? They want to possess you entirely. They want to take everything from you and there I am standing naked, as it were. Well, I can't give anymore. They say those who give will get. They say that the more you give the more you get. Do you believe that? That's philosophy, that's what that is. But, as I was saying, he's not happy either. He's bored, too. He's never got enough either. No one ever has enough. We all want everything. Everything of what? I ask you . . . life? . . . hah, life. But I won't bother you any longer. I did rattle on at you didn't I? Have you ever had anyone speak to you like that before? Oh, if you only knew. Nothing pleases my husband. Nothing, ever. Me neither, now that I think of it. Oh, we're all the same. And they say there's a God somewhere. And the thought of those who are worse off than you is consoling for a while, but then you start getting depressed at all those poor slobs living with all that misery. If you keep thinking of them, you get dizzy, you could lose your footing and fall to their level. Oh, that's something I couldn't take, let me tell you, poverty. And yet, and yet, there's a blue sky some-where. There's a gray sky, too, of course. Then, there's everything else. And newspapers, and politics. I don't enjoy the newspapers, myself. And politics isn't very amusing either, that's for sure. Those who have too much and those who don't have enough. Me, I don't have enough. You see what happens the instant you start looking down. It's much better to keep looking up. Noth-ing is worth anything, let me tell you. We're so bored, so bored. How can we get so bored? You will come to our get-togethers, won't you? We'll be so happy to have you. We know how to make you feel at home. Well, goodbye for now. (*She starts to go to the door.*) See you soon? (*She's in the doorway, and turns.*) And don't forget . . . be careful of the concierge.

She exits.

SCENE VI

The CHARACTER's *apartment.*

The CHARACTER; the HUSBAND OF THE WOMAN WITH THE
DOG.

The CHARACTER *throws his coat into a corner, along with
his hat. He sits down in the chair, seemingly exhausted,
and jumps up abruptly at the entrance of . . . a man, the*
HUSBAND *of the* WOMAN WITH THE DOG, *who enters from
the doorway.*

HUSBAND: How do you do, sir, I'm disturbing you perhaps.
Oh, I know I'm disturbing you. Oh, you're too polite

to say so, I know. Or is it that I'm not disturbing you at all. My wife just left your apartment. She must have told you a lot of things. That's why I'm here. I came to get to know you. We have to know each other in order to be able to help each other. I don't want to get you involved with confidential matters. But, she's crazy. What must she have told you! Oh, I'm very discreet. I won't say anything. You ought to know something, though, she's a woman who doesn't like life. Never satisfied. She says it's the others who aren't satisfied. It's not true. She doesn't know what to do anymore. Life is terrible with women like that. She doesn't want to have any children. I was willing. She did everything she could to avoid them. I used to tell her that if she had children, she'd be less bored. She agreed but said we should try dogs first. So she went out and got a whole litter. I don't like animals myself, I prefer children, but I guess I don't really hate animals either. She poisoned them, sir. Luckily they were not children, she would have done the same thing. She'd be in prison this very minute. I told her, "Aren't you happy to have escaped prison? You're much better off here in your own home. That should comfort you." No, she's still bored. You want to be strong, you want to be a man, but sometimes it gets to be too much. You've got to be reasonable with people who have lost their reason. She organizes get-togethers at the house. With neighbors, inside the house and out. They play cards and she always wants to win. She doesn't play for money, but she wants to win anyway. Oh, she likes money too, don't worry. What does she do with it, would you like to know? She puts it into piggy banks she's got all over the house. She has tantrums and breaks dishes, tears the drapes, throws things on the parquet floors to filthy them up. She does that sort of thing in front of her guests during her reunions, yes! She yells at them. At first they laugh, but then it's not so funny and, when they go, they don't come back. So she invites new ones. That's no doubt the reason she came up here to see you. She's looking for new blood. She's exhausting the possibilities of this neighborhood. When no one wants to accept her invitations, she goes out, she has lovers, I don't know where she finds them, she's so ugly. Mind you, it doesn't bother me, I've worked things out for myself. Each time she finds someone, she's sure she'll never be bored again. But she's bored anyway, always and with everyone. Other times she laughs hysterically. The minute she starts that laughing, I'm not happy because I know what's coming. She breaks as many dishes when she's laughing as she does when she's angry; it helps keep her up, I suppose. You think I ought to have her looked at. I've thought of that myself. She's seen lots of doctors. There was one who gave up outright. She jumped all over him. He committed suicide. She passed her craziness on to him. And he was a shrink, you'd think he could cope with it. But he was as crazy as the crazies he treated. Treating crazy people is no joke. It's contagious, like a virus. I'm not saying all this to keep you from coming to her little bridge gettogethers. But you'll see for yourself. Me, I look for my own friends, my own pals. I like going down to the corner bar for a drink every now and then. I'll take you along one day. There're a couple of good bars in the neighborhood. But her, I don't know what's the matter with her, so help me. I'm sure it wouldn't take much to cure her. One word, maybe. But which? But don't let her turn you around. I'm not saying that out of jealousy, believe me. I don't care about that, I told you. I'm just warning you for your own good. She'll drive you crazy. You look like a calm man, well balanced, adjusted, you look healthy. She'll drive you nuts. When she goes into one of her fits, she could tear down brick walls. Apartments become neurotic. Furniture, waiters in restaurants. We'll go out of the area . . . I have a car. We'll have a few drinks, nothing serious. I don't like drinking much, but it's relaxing. What do you say? Eh, what do you say? Oh, I don't mean to bully you. I'll be going, I am disturbing you, I can tell. It's my wife's pushiness that's catching. Come and see us just the same. We'll have a good time. Well, goodbye. See you soon. Oh, just between us, watch out for the concierge. (*He leaves. He returns an instant later.*) My wife is a terrible cook. And they say everything is the man's fault.

He leaves for good. The CHARACTER *sits down on the chair. Someone else comes in. He again jumps abruptly to his feet.*

SCENE VII

The CHARACTER's *apartment.*

The CHARACTER; A MAN.

From the entrance door a gray-haired MAN *limps in on his cane. He could be speaking with a Russian accent.*

MAN: Forgive me for dropping in on you unannounced this way. Ah, I see that you have a chair. If you don't mind, I'll take it. I have trouble staying upright. I came to make your acquaintance. We must get acquainted, after all. We must all get to know each other if we are to appreciate each other. Only once you know someone

can you begin to like him or at least find him likeable.
I find you likeable already. I like to be friendly with
people. What would we do if we couldn't be friendly
with one another? The reason we have wars is that countries don't know each other well enough. Or because we
don't know each other at all. I know about wars, my
friend. You've noticed that I have a limp. . . . Well,
I'm one of the many war-wounded. Well we made war
on people we didn't know and with whom we couldn't
get along just because they spoke a language we didn't
understand. If we had learned to speak it, if they had
learned to speak ours, if we had met before, we would no
doubt not have been at war with each other. In a word,
I shall not be in your way much longer, but I am a cripple for the rest of my life. It's tragic, my friend, tragic.
I don't read newspapers anymore. They make me too unhappy. Just glance at the papers . . . I can't do it anymore. There are killings, murders, epidemics, floods,
insects, earthquakes, genocides, fires, tyrannies. What do
they all have against each other? The explanations they
give us: man exploiting man, social injustice, economic
crisis . . . all that seems hardly justification enough for
universal massacres. Ideology, demands for rights, these
can't explain everything, they hardly deserve the cata-
clysms they provoke. Ideologies are outrun by violence,
they are merely a pretext for violence. A mystery. Everything is a mystery. And everything is violence. We were
taught "Love thy neighbor." Actually it should have
been "Devour thy neighbor." In fact that's exactly what
"Love thy neighbor" means. We devour what we love.
The world is badly conceived. The one who conceived
it did not succeed. We're obliged to eat, we live in a

closed-circuit economy. Nothing arrives from elsewhere and we must keep eating, eating ourselves, to stay alive. Just look into a microscope and you'll see what happens in the cells: microscopic beings keep eating each other, since everything must stay alive. But why do we have to have this desire to live? Because the creature who thought up this bloody world wanted his creation to survive. So he instilled in us the desire to live and that means the need to devour each other because, as I said, we live in a closed-circuit economy. If we could only cease desiring to live, it would all come to an end. But HE doesn't want it to end. So he keeps us like that, alive, surviving, with our desires exploding within us. I have tried to quiet the desires in me. Desire for everything, for anything, for nothing. The desire for nothing is still desire. The desire to come see you is still a desire and as such is unhealthy. Well, unhealthy is perhaps too strong. In fact it's inaccurate because, once I know you, I no longer can desire to devour you. Don't you agree that we live in a kind of hell? That hell is right here. We are all hungry, thirsty, desirous, and as soon as we've gratified our hunger, like our thirst, like our desires, there are other desires, and hungers, and thirsts. There is the fertile imagination which will keep inventing as it goes along, clever little devil that it is. But one mustn't give in to it. We are slaves of our desires, we rely on each other, we always expect someone to satisfy our desires. Everyone expects everything from everyone else. If I could only keep myself from drinking water, or eating bread. It ought to be possible. I've tried not to eat or drink for three days, but I didn't last longer than that. We ought to be able to commit suicide. But it's not easy because HE also gave us an instinct for self-preservation, the fear of death. He has protected us against ourselves. He invented fear. To tell the truth, I'm afraid of everything. You, don't you feel threatened? I feel especially afraid when there's nothing to be afraid of. I'm always wondering what's coming next. There must be something preparing itself in silence, during the truce! I have the feeling that the walls are vibrating. That an earthquake is in the making. I think that objects have been replaced by other objects which look alike and yet are not. These substitutions must take place constantly. The chair I'm sitting on this instant is not the same one I sat on upon entering here. Everything is moving constantly. Everything is falling to pieces. Sometimes I can hear the cracking, sometimes not, but it's always going on, the insidious cracking and the moving around. It's strange. It's always the same and yet always a little different. Why is He doing that? Any second it could all split in half. I'm amazed it hasn't happened already. I keep waiting for it. Don't think I'm talking like a fool, I'm not a fool, I'm calm and collected. But even I cannot adapt to everything. And who is the real wise man in the long run? The one who accepts everything or the one who decides to reject everything? Is resignation an act of wisdom? At times I'm tempted to think that wisdom is another form of madness. If we at least had the possibility of finding out certain facts. But we can know nothing, we remain ignorant. We have been deprived of the possibility of conceiving this world because we cannot conceive the finite nor the infinite nor the un-finite nor the non-infinite. We live in a kind of prison which is a box. This box is enclosed in another box, which is boxed into another box, boxed into another box, and so on, ad infinitum. And infinity, as I was saying, is something we cannot conceive. Everything is inconceivable. The greats of science knew no more about it than we do. The very idea of not being able to even imagine the universe from one end to the other—or that which we can call one end to the other, since the universe is perhaps without end. At least to be able to imagine a non-end. We were made not to know. I know only one thing and one thing only, and that is that I cannot know. I can know nothing. Well, I cannot accept that. But HE doesn't care that I can't accept that, because he made us the way we are, so that we cannot know, DELIBERATELY. And yet we go on building, yes, building planes, cannons, rockets, electricity, spaceships. We go on with our handiwork. We work at our trivia within the realm of the inexplicable. The inextricable. What a mess. Well, we shall be seeing each other, sir, sooner or later, at least I hope so. I shall be going now. We'll talk about all this some other time. I have confidence in you, you'll bring me insights, I'm sure. (*He gets up, starts to go.*) Goodbye, sir. Oh yes, a last word: Watch out for the concierge.

He exits.

SCENE VIII

The CHARACTER's *apartment.*

The CHARACTER; *the* CONCIERGE.

The CHARACTER *goes over to the chair and sits down. He remains for a long moment without moving. After a while, he raises his head, looks at the ceiling, then the floor, then all around him. Slowly he gets up and goes toward his right. His shoes squeak against the floor boards. He looks like a frightened creature. He bends down and feels his shoes, then feels the floor. Slowly, on the tips of his feet, he presses his hand against the right wall to get the feel of its thickness. Raises his shoulders in a gesture which seems to say, "Well, that's solid enough." He goes to the rear wall, repeats the same gestures. Then does the same with the left wall. This time he touches it first gently, then firmly, then pushes it with all his strength. Then he pulls back suddenly. Steps back even more. He waits a few moments. He shrugs his shoulders.*

CHARACTER: It'll hold up.

He goes to stage center. Looks at the ceiling.

And that?

He shrugs again but looks less certain this time. He goes abruptly to where he dropped his coat and hat. He goes through his pockets, takes out a package of cigarettes, then, on tiptoe, sneaks back to the chair where he tries to sit down. He hesitates. He makes sure that the chair is sturdy and doesn't wobble. He sits down, settles back. He lights a cigarette and remains comfortably seated as he smokes.

I didn't think of that.

A few moments of silence. Looks around to see where he can toss his cigarette butt. He finally decides to throw it on the floor, squashes it with his foot, looks up at the ceiling again.

Must put a light up there.

He takes out his package of cigarettes from his pocket, pulls out one, puts the package back into his pocket.

Mustn't overdo it.

He gets up, remains motionless a few instants, facing the

audience. Suddenly he starts jumping up and down and, just as suddenly, he stops.

Yeah, that'll hold.

He stays put a few seconds, then runs to stage left front, where he appears to have found a window. He pulls back an imaginary curtain and looks out at the audience, that is, into the street below.

That's it.

Silence.

It's okay.

Silence.

It's lively.

He pulls away from the window, walks around the apartment, his hands behind his back, a couple of times, as though he were inspecting the premises. He disappears for a moment in the back. We hear him walking around the other rooms. He returns after a minute or two. He settles back into his chair, takes out his package of cigarettes, takes one and lights it, looks around blankly . . . all this very slowly, his face without expression.

The CONCIERGE *arrives. She is a woman in her forties with a gentle air about her.*

CONCIERGE: Good day, sir, I'm the concierge.

The CHARACTER *swings around with a look of apprehension on his face. Turns to face the* CONCIERGE. *She faces front.*

How are you, sir. Your furniture has arrived. It's downstairs. They'll be bringing it up in a couple of minutes.

You've got a lot of furniture. You'll certainly be making a lot of friends in the neighborhood. There's no point living alone like a bear. Here we have good people and some not so good people. But you, with the set-up you've got, you can be happy. You've got to live with a little joy in your heart. With a little sunshine in your soul, things become brighter and younger, even if the sky is gray. That's what I try to do anyway. To be alive is beautiful. I'll find you a maid to keep the place clean. You probably don't even know how to use a vacuum cleaner. You know what I've discovered, sir? Everything is surprising. I listen to a lot of people talk, in fact I like listening to them. It's a little bit a part of my business, since I'm a concierge. And besides, I've got to admit, I'm curious. Well, there's always something interesting in what they say, even when they talk nonsense. They're part of the world, and they have their own world full of events: comedies, mysteries, crises. But there's always a story to tell: they went on a trip, they would have liked to go on a trip, they never made a trip. They were wounded in the war, they were ambushed, they had accidents, children were born. Their old folks died, others get born, it begins all over. That's the way it is, things wilt and things bud. And you're especially lucky to be in our area because, since we're a southern suburb, the weather is warmer and sunnier than in the center of the city or in the northern suburb. You know, it makes no difference if you're rich or a bum . . . the gift of joy can happen to anybody. Even ugliness can be beautiful, sadness can turn to gladness. The frost of Siberia cannot withstand the warmth of the heart. Naturally you have to know which button to press to make the world light up. Well the next time you walk past my door, just pop in if you've got a minute, so we can talk a little. Don't you like to talk? Well, I'll be going. Your furniture is here.

We hear noise. The CONCIERGE *exits. She returns with a crate.*

Your bottles arrived first. No, sir, I don't touch alcohol.

She puts down the crate which the CHARACTER *will put inside a sideboard which will arrive later.*

I'll be going now, sir. I've got to take care of my dog and season my soup. Sound boring? You have no idea how absorbing a little dog and a pot of soup can be. Ah, there I go again, I do rattle on, don't I? But now I'm really off. Oh, one last thing, but strictly between us, eh? Watch out for the lady with the poodle. You can't imagine how mean she is, a real snake, and her husband's no better. And the Russian who came to see you, I've been told that he's a spy. Anyway, he looks like one; I believe it. Look out for people who say they like you two seconds after they've met you. They want to grab you, hold you in their claws, strangle you, kill you. But don't you worry, aside from that, they're all nice enough. I didn't say what I did just to bad-mouth them. Don't think that, please. I just wanted to put you on your guard, without worrying you. They could turn out to be good friends some day. If you're interested, and if you're discreet, I'll let you in on a lot more. No, no brandy, I told you, I never touch it. Only a little absinthe every now and then, that's different.

She exits.

SCENE IX

The CHARACTER's *apartment.*

The CHARACTER.

We hear a noise coming from upstage. The CHARACTER *gets up and goes toward the noise. We see a large yellow sideboard appear. The* CHARACTER *goes to the sideboard, which is on wheels. He pushes it against the wall, stage right. He steps back, looks at the sideboard longingly, then seems satisfied with its placement. He opens it, takes out a bottle of cognac, a glass, pours a drink, and then downs it. He puts back the bottle, thinks better of it, pours another* drink and downs it. Then he replaces both bottle and glass.

We hear another noise and see a round table appear from upstage, also on wheels. The CHARACTER pushes the table to stage center, contemplates it with satisfaction, wipes off the dust with his hand even though the surface appears brand-new and immaculate. Then again from upstage, six chairs appear one after the other and with a steady, unhurried rhythm, he places each around the table. He steps back and takes in sideboard, chairs, and table. Earlier he moved the first chair, which was stage center front, to a corner, stage left. Again from the back a red round rug arrives and, after trying clumsily to lift chairs and table so as to place it on the floor, he gives up and leaves it lying on the table. Four more chairs arrive and two of these he places on either side of the sideboard. From stage left roll in two armchairs, one blue and the other violet. He places them downstage at the place where the window is supposed to be. As though he were trying them out, he sits first in one then the other. Then he goes over to the table and tries out each of the six chairs there. From upstage a rolled-up canvas arrives. He unrolls it and hangs it on the upstage wall. The picture should be big enough for the audience to be able to make out the subject: A papa dog, mama dog, and puppy dog, all cocker spaniels. A guéridon (pedestal table) arrives from upstage. As the CHARACTER grabs it, he looks around to find an appropriate place for it. He decides to put it between the two armchairs. Another guéridon arrives; this he places stage center. A case arrives, out of which he takes three vases, one at a time: one for the table, one for the first guéridon and the other for the second guéridon. A huge green sofa appears from upstage. He places this behind the armchairs. Then he changes his mind and he puts the two armchairs behind the sofa, then again he changes them to one on either side of the sofa. Another crate arrives and he takes out a floor lamp with an orange shade. He plugs it in, observes the light, then he turns it off, then he relights it, then he turns it off again. From the curtain rods huge drapes and curtains fall into place; these are bright red with black leaves. He pulls them back and ties them into place. A pendulum clock comes out from upstage. He places this next to the sideboard. With a kick he knocks the empty crates upstage. He looks around at everything, piece after piece, goes over to sit on the sofa, then lies back. He puts his hands behind his head and whistles softly. He stops whistling, he closes his eyes, stretches his arms down next to his body. He closes his eyes. He remains like this without moving for a few seconds. Then suddenly he gets up and goes toward the sideboard, takes the cognac bottle out again, with the glass, pours a drink, drinks it down, and another, then puts both back; he skips around from one piece of furniture to another, looks out the window, then disappears upstage. After a long moment during which the stage remains encumbered with furniture but empty of life, we hear a noise in the background; he is walking around and humming. He reappears from upstage, a cloth in his hand, and he begins to wax the floor, under the table, the chairs, in the empty spaces. He takes out a flask from his back pocket and takes a swallow from it. He replaces this in his back pocket. He waxes on. The curtain comes down.

A Hell of a Mess

Alternative ending for Scene IX.

The curtain can come down at this point or there can simply be a blackout. If an intermission is placed here, the curtain would come down. If there is merely a blackout, we will hear at once the following noises. If there is an intermission, these noises will be heard during the blackout before the next scene begins.

We hear the sounds of buses moving in the streets, motor bikes and Vespas, street cries such as: "Hey, watch out," "Watcha thinkya doing," whistles, a street fight between a man and a woman, screams, strident laughter, a horn, a siren, sounds of crowds moving in the streets. More words, real or invented, etc.

SCENE X

The dining room of a small restaurant on the outskirts of town.

A couple, an OLD MAN *and an* OLD WOMAN; *two* MEN; *a* WAITRESS/AGNES; *the* PROPRIETOR; *the* CHARACTER, *the* FIRST REVOLUTIONARY, *the* SECOND REVOLUTIONARY, *the* THIRD REVOLUTIONARY, *the* WOMAN REVOLUTIONARY. *Big dolls can pose as other people.*

The PROPRIETOR *is behind the bar. A man is seated alone at the bar. Two or three other tables are around in which the dolls can be seated. (This device to be used in case there are not enough actors for extras.) A huge mirror can* be used to give the impression that the restaurant has even more customers. At stage center there is a little table which is empty. For a long moment, people eat in silence. Also in silence, the WAITRESS moves back from the kitchen door, upstage right, to the tables, serving food and carrying empty plates. We hear the muted sounds of street traffic in the background outside the restaurant. The man at the bar finishes his drink, then goes over to a table and sits down. A few murmurs are heard, then silence again.

The restaurant door opens with a slight creak, and the CHARACTER enters. He takes a few embarrassed steps to stage center and looks around him. The WAITRESS comes up to greet him. She is still young, pleasant-looking, and has a nice figure despite posture which indicates fatigue.

CHARACTER: Good evening.

PROPRIETOR: Good evening, sir.

The other diners pay no attention to the CHARACTER.

WAITRESS: Dinner, sir?

The CHARACTER nods yes, then he points to the small table downstage center.

WAITRESS: Why of course, sir, you may sit there if you like.

The CHARACTER thanks her with a nod of the head again, then he goes over to sit down. Then he gets up to hang his hat on an old-fashioned clothes horse. He sits down again as the WAITRESS brings him the menu. He takes it silently.

WAITRESS: Would you like a drink?

The CHARACTER *nods yes.*

What would you like—Campari, Pernod, or hard liquor?

CHARACTER: Not uh hard.

WAITRESS: Campari or Pernod, then. The Campari is nice and cool.

CHARACTER: Campari.

WAITRESS: With ice and soda?

CHARACTER: With ice only . . . a double . . . please.

WAITRESS: And to eat?

He's silent, then he consults the menu and looks undecided.

WAITRESS: I suggest the sardines to start with. Okay? Fine. A sardine to start. And then?

He looks just as undecided.

A steak? Or beef Burgundy?

CHARACTER: Steak. No, beef. No, steak, well done.

WAITRESS: With fries? Fine, with fries it is.

CHARACTER: And Camembert after that.

WAITRESS: Oh, take the Brie, it's much better tonight, nice and ripe.

CHARACTER: I'll have Brie.

WAITRESS: Will you have dessert? Well, you can decide that later. Would you like some wine with your meal? I recommend the Beaujolais, it's from the boss' special reserve.

CHARACTER: A half bottle.

WAITRESS: I'll bring your Campari right over.

She returns with the aperitif, which he drinks in one gulp.

CHARACTER: Another please.

WAITRESS: Already?

CHARACTER: I'm thirsty. Thank you. And a full bottle of Beaujolais, not a half.

The WAITRESS *brings his second drink, then goes away to see to his order. The* CHARACTER *puts his elbows on the table, holding his face in his hands for a moment. Then he drinks his second Campari in one shot.*

CHARACTER: One more.

WAITRESS: Not so fast, sir, that stuff packs a punch too, you know.

CHARACTER: Three's my ration, I'm used to it.

The Campari doesn't seem to have affected the CHARAC-TER. *However, he suddenly seems more relaxed. His face appears contented. He looks around him smilingly, especially toward the audience, where the main street is supposed to run and which he is supposed to be able to see through the restaurant windows. We see the* PRO-PRIETOR *finish a drink all by himself at the bar.*

During this time the WAITRESS *is moving around silently, serving both real and dummy customers. Every-*

one eats in silence. We hear a street noise every now and then. Slowly the scene becomes surreal as the WAITRESS' movements become slower as in a strange dance (a kind of slow-motion sequence). The diners' eating motions are slowed down also. The street noises become less strident, almost musical.

CHARACTER: It's strange, all these people. (*To the* WAITRESS, *showing her his empty glass.*) One more, please.

WAITRESS: Right away.

The CHARACTER *looks around him again.*

CHARACTER: All these people . . .

OLD MAN (*to the* OLD WOMAN): Did you like the paté?

CHARACTER (*looking out toward the audience again*): All those girls . . . all those young people . . . old people . . . all that activity.

OLD MAN (*to* OLD WOMAN): Where are we going? We're governed by fools. With leaders like ours, you can't go far . . .

FIRST MAN (*alone at his table*): We'll go too far, on the contrary. You'll see, one fine day they won't be happy with the results of their tricks.

The OLD MAN *and* WOMAN *look at the* FIRST MAN, *then look down at their plates.*

OLD WOMAN (*to the* OLD MAN): I don't know what to do. Have you already done it?

SECOND MAN (*to the* FIRST MAN): Oh I sure have!

The WAITRESS *arrives with a tray full of orders. She places this on the table.*

WAITRESS: Here is your Campari, sir, and your Beaujolais. Your steak and your cheese. (*She sets the table and lays out the plates in a kindly, protective fashion.*) You're too eager.

The CHARACTER *grabs the Campari and downs it in one shot.*

You drink too fast and too much, if I may say so, sir. It's bad for you.

CHARACTER: Oh no.

WAITRESS: You know, the wine here is really very good. Our drinks too. And our food is always fresh. In fact we're the best restaurant around; all the cooking is done by the proprietor on the premises. All our clients eat here with enthusiasm. There is a kind of late-night snack place which has a kind of snappy, with-it look, but nobody ever goes there.

CHARACTER (*after finishing his drink*): No, it's not bad for me. I'd like to come here every day. Can you reserve the same table for me?

WAITRESS: You like your little habits, I see. In a small restaurant like this we don't reserve. But if you'd like, I'll ask the boss.

She goes over to the PROPRIETOR *and discusses the situation with him silently. He nods yes. Meanwhile, the* CHARACTER *has poured himself some wine. The other diners keep their heads down, facing their plates.*

CHARACTER (*after finishing his glass of wine*): Everything's clearer now.

The WAITRESS *returns to the* CHARACTER.

WAITRESS: Yes, sir, the boss says it's okay. Every day at 12:30, the same table.

CHARACTER: Who are you?

WAITRESS: My name is Agnes. I'm the boss' sister-in-law. A cousin of mine works here too. The boss does all the buying.

CHARACTER: But who are you?

WAITRESS: I told you, I'm Agnes, waitress here, in this restaurant.

CHARACTER: Are you sure?

AGNES: Oh yes, quite sure.

CHARACTER: Do you think things will last indefinitely? You don't think things will fall apart any minute, do you?

AGNES: How could things fall apart?

CHARACTER: Just like that, all of a sudden. Who can guarantee that it won't happen?

AGNES: When we're all long gone things will still be the same. Don't you worry about it one bit.

CHARACTER: Do you see them passing in the street? Isn't it strange?

AGNES: It's not the first time you've seen that!

CHARACTER: Yes it is, I see everything for the first time. All around me everything is turning and turning. Seeing a lot of people like that . . . crowds . . . it's comforting.

All of a sudden a spot from above illuminates the CHARACTER's *table.*

Oh, how extraordinary. What do you think of that?

AGNES: It's just a ray of light.

CHARACTER (*pausing after each phrase*): It changes everything . . . it's strange . . . strange . . . brand new . . . (*very faintly*) we are elsewhere.

AGNES: Excuse me, sir, I have work to do. No, no, don't worry, I'll be back.

She goes about her work. A change has come about in the atmosphere of the restaurant. The light has become more luminous everywhere. The CHARACTER *gets up, sits down, gets up again.*

FIRST MAN (*seated at one of the tables*): Miss, my mushrooms, please.

The voices and motions are a little out of step, orders are given in a sing-songy way and the walking is a dance step again.

OLD MAN (*getting up and sitting down*): Our sausage, please.

SECOND MAN: My potato salad, please.

CHARACTER: Potatoes, how nice. And here I am with all this, forks, plates, knives. (*Ecstatic.*)

We hear the melodious sound of cutlery.

PROPRIETOR (*singing*): They are beautiful, they are good. What is good is beautiful.

CHARACTER: The Beaujolais is magnificent.

PROPRIETOR (*singing*): Wine is sun in a bottle.

WAITRESS (*dancing and singing in a circle*): I'm coming, be patient, everything comes in due time.

The light becomes brighter and brighter.

OLD WOMAN: Everything comes . . . isn't that wonderful.

FIRST MAN (*to the* PROPRIETOR): I'll buy you a drink.

He goes to the bar and has a drink with the PROPRIETOR.

I should get back to work, but I'm in no hurry.

The CHARACTER *points his empty bottle at the* WAITRESS.

WAITRESS: You want another one? Don't you think that's too much?

CHARACTER: No, today I'm celebrating.

OLD MAN (*still singing*): I've been retired for fifteen years now.

WAITRESS: And here's our wine.

OLD WOMAN: But we're still very much alive.

CHARACTER: And a coffee, please.

SECOND MAN: Ah, if only every day was Sunday.

OLD MAN: It's never the same thing.

PROPRIETOR (*to the* FIRST MAN): Another drink; it's my turn.

The WAITRESS *brings the Beaujolais and the coffee, and leaves.*

FIRST MAN: With pleasure, thank you.

OLD MAN: Three more, that makes nine.

He gets up.

FIRST MAN (*to the* WAITRESS): Won't you have a drink with us?

CHARACTER: There's this, all this, it's wonderful.

WAITRESS: I'm sorry, sir, I can't. As you can see, I've got my hands full, serving customers. I'll have a drink with you later.

FIRST MAN (*looking toward the audience in a state of euphoria*): You don't often see the sun at this time of the year.

OLD WOMAN (*getting up*): That depends.

They all rise and look toward the audience. The light moves from bright back to gray quickly. The old couple and the others turn around and sit back down. The FIRST MAN *goes back to his place also. The dancing motion of the people walking grinds to a halt. The* CHARACTER *sits down finally. The sing-song quality of the talking becomes a murmur, then silence. Everyone has become quiet. The silhouettes of the diners have become forlorn-looking once more. Suddenly the* CHARACTER *gets up.*

CHARACTER (*the sound of the plates is no longer melodious*): We're back here again!

The customers look at each other with surprise, then go on eating.

They're all back in their glass coffin. (*To the* WAITRESS) Everything's dim and gray again. The magic's gone.

WAITRESS: Nothing's gone. What are you talking about? Everything's the same. You don't look so good. Aren't you feeling well? I'll bring you a brandy.

CHARACTER (*to the* WAITRESS): Do we have skin?

The WAITRESS *moves over to him and observes him a moment without reacting, then she walks away.*

What are they all about (*looking toward the audience, that is, out the front door and windows of the restaurant at the people in the street*), all that moving around? All that hustle and bustle. Where are they all going?

No reaction from the audience.

Can't you understand? Someone put the lid back on.

He sits down. The customers continue to eat in silence. We hear the sound of plates and silverware. Everything has become sluggish again, lifeless.

Agnes, Agnes, you are part of the mist!

Suddenly, we hear the roar of motorcycles outside, carrying revolutionaries. If the director desires, we could see the silhouettes of their motorcycles in the background. The instant their motors stop screaming, they break into the restaurant, noisily.

CHARACTER: That is no longer mist. It's iron and stone and lead. And motors, more motors.

The FIRST REVOLUTIONARY *steps into the back of the restaurant, a band around his head. A* SECOND REVOLUTIONARY *slips in. A* THIRD REVOLUTIONARY *enters straight into the restaurant; a rifle strapped to his shoulder, he goes to the bar with a quick, determined step. The customers, after looking up at the intrusion, have gone back to eating monotonously.*

THIRD REVOLUTIONARY (*military fashion*): Gimme a whiskey. I've just come from a skirmish, I'm thirsty and hot.

A small WOMAN *enters, part of the gang. She's tight-lipped and nervous. She goes to the bar.*

WOMAN REVOLUTIONARY: A whiskey!

The eaters turn their heads to look at the pair.

THIRD REVOLUTIONARY: They're fighting in the town square.

Little by little the eaters become interested in the pair. One by one they get up from their tables and go over to encircle them.

OLD MAN: We've never heard of anything like that before.

WOMAN REVOLUTIONARY: Haven't you heard the explosions?

Everyone listens attentively, turning in the same direction. In the distance, we hear noises of battle.

OLD WOMAN: Yes, indeed.

OLD MAN: It certainly is coming from the town square. I go there every Sunday for my Sunday walk. Last Sunday all was calm. Will it be over by next Sunday?

OLD WOMAN: Of course it will, dear. These things never last long.

PROPRIETOR: There really is a lot of fighting going on out there. Here we go again. Things have been quiet too long I guess.

REVOLUTIONARY: It won't be over by Sunday, Grandpa!

OLD MAN: Then I won't have my Sunday walk?

WOMAN REVOLUTIONARY: Soon every day will be Sunday. That's what we're fighting for.

OLD MAN: In the meantime, I won't have my Sunday.

FIRST REVOLUTIONARY: If there's fighting, it's already Sunday.

SECOND REVOLUTIONARY: Is it for good this time?

PROPRIETOR: It's downtown too.

WAITRESS: It's only in our suburb.

THIRD REVOLUTIONARY: We don't give a shit about downtown. Fuck the rich.

WOMAN REVOLUTIONARY: For the time being we're sticking to our neighborhood. There's enough cleaning up to do right here.

Slowly the intensity of the situation, the fighting sounds outside, increase. During the scene we see guerrillas running with rifles, then civilians running in flight. The sounds get louder and we see people with blood streaming down their faces or bodies. We see policemen chasing guerrillas. We will hear singing and shouting, building up to the culmination of the scene.

SECOND MAN: I don't understand any of this.

WAITRESS: What kind of a life is this?

WOMAN REVOLUTIONARY (*looking at them with scorn*): It's a good thing there are still real men around! (*She slaps the* THIRD REVOLUTIONARY *on the back.*) Without guys like you, we'd really be in trouble. We'll get 'em all, eh?

THIRD REVOLUTIONARY: We've got to.

PROPRIETOR (*to the* THIRD REVOLUTIONARY): Another drink, it's on the house!

OLD MAN: I was in a revolution too, when I was young, in Sardinia.

OLD WOMAN: My husband is an ex-anarchist!

FIRST MAN: I can understand that you're disgusted with the way things are, I mean, the way things were, provided that they don't stay the way they are . . .

PROPRIETOR: Yes, yes, I understand you, too. It's society's fault.

Toward the end of the scene, the two MEN *clients of the restaurant, the* OLD MAN *and* WOMAN, *will become* REVOLUTIONARIES *also. At the very end, just before exiting, they will change clothes, will have guns and bullet belts, will wear beards and wigs appropriate to their new roles.*

OLD MAN: In my day, in '48, I did my duty, yes indeed. Now, I'd rather be left alone to die in peace and quiet.

OLD WOMAN: Oh we're not going to lose any sleep over this, dear.

SECOND MAN: We're sophisticated, after all. We're French.

PROPRIETOR: France is a country of revolutionaries, like Mexico. There was '89, then there was '37, '47, '57, '67, '77, '87 and again '89.

OLD MAN: The cycle is complete.

THIRD REVOLUTIONARY: There's no such thing as a cycle. There's no such thing as complete! The pigs!

While the others have grouped around the REVOLUTIONARIES, *the* CHARACTER *is the only one standing by himself.*

THIRD REVOLUTIONARY: It's now or never.

WOMAN REVOLUTIONARY: We've got to make them face the facts.

WAITRESS: They'll face the facts, all right.

FIRST MAN: Things have got to change.

PROPRIETOR: Let's drink to that, on the house everybody.

SECOND MAN: Bravo!

OLD WOMAN: Bravo, young man.

WAITRESS (*to the* CHARACTER): Don't bother coming over, I'll bring you your glass.

OLD WOMAN: You're going to serve him?

WAITRESS: Why not, he's a customer.

She brings him his glass and returns to the group.

THIRD REVOLUTIONARY: Things couldn't go on the way they were.

OLD WOMAN: With men like you around . . .

OLD MAN: You've got to go to the core of things. Oh, if only I were your age again.

THIRD REVOLUTIONARY: It's a country of slugs, a sick society.

OLD WOMAN: We're sick to death of it.

EVERYONE: Oh, we sure are.

FIRST MAN: They deserve nothing but scorn.

SECOND MAN: Scorn is not enough.

WOMAN REVOLUTIONARY: We've got to be through with it. We've got to draw blood. Justice will be served by our lust for blood.

THIRD REVOLUTIONARY: We'll eliminate them. It'll be better for everyone.

PROPRIETOR: That's right.

THIRD REVOLUTIONARY: We'll be fair.

WOMAN REVOLUTIONARY: Fair but stern. Justice has its price, they'll find that out.

OLD WOMAN: All those who wallowed in debauchery and opportunism.

OLD MAN: They were ignorant and dangerous.

WAITRESS: Oh yes, very dangerous.

PROPRIETOR: They were certainly very dangerous and ignorant.

FIRST MAN: They were ignorant of everything.

THIRD REVOLUTIONARY: Here's to the class struggle.

OLD WOMAN: To the butcher of Red Square.

WAITRESS: No mercy to the oppressors!

FIRST MAN: No mercy to the rich!

SECOND MAN: Here's to the poor!

PROPRIETOR: To the proletariat!

THIRD REVOLUTIONARY: To dictatorship but with liberty for all.

OLD WOMAN: As long as everyone has a vote on it.

PROPRIETOR: Everyone will.

OLD MAN: To happy tomorrows.

WOMAN REVOLUTIONARY: To the oppressors' sorrows.

WAITRESS: It'll be another St. Bartholomew's night.

WOMAN REVOLUTIONARY: We'll demand our dues in blood.

WAITRESS: They deserve it, with all their corruption.

FIRST MAN: The rotten rich.

OLD WOMAN: The workers are poor because they drink; they're all alcoholics.

SECOND MAN: What about drugs?

PROPRIETOR: Consumer's society!

OLD WOMAN: Collectivism, individualism!

WAITRESS: Our consumer society!

FIRST MAN: The drinkers of the people's blood.

SECOND MAN: All of them sell-outs!

THIRD REVOLUTIONARY (*in a blood-thirsty shout, banging his fist on the counter and sending glasses flying*): What about brotherhood? Damn it, don't forget brotherhood!

There is silence for a moment; everyone seems a bit frightened.

PROPRIETOR (*to the* WAITRESS): Start cleaning up.

The WAITRESS *begins. The conversations resume.*

WOMAN REVOLUTIONARY: We'll shove it down their throats with our fists, with our knives. We'll slit their throats with it.

OLD WOMAN: We're sick and tired.

OLD MAN: He was right about what he said just now . . . we mustn't forget brotherhood.

WAITRESS: We mustn't forget brotherhood.

FIRST MAN: We mustn't forget brotherhood.

SECOND MAN: No, we mustn't forget brotherhood.

PROPRIETOR: Not brotherhood.

OLD WOMAN: Three-quarters of the world lives in poverty.

PROPRIETOR: We're privileged compared to them.

THIRD REVOLUTIONARY: We're not privileged in relationship to our privileges.

FIRST MAN: No more privileges!

SECOND MAN: Down with privileges!

WOMAN REVOLUTIONARY: Blood! Bayonets in their bellies. I want to see their guts on the ground.

WAITRESS: Human nature is the same.

OLD MAN: Revolutions pass. Evolution or revolution, it all passes.

WAITRESS: Everything has an end and a beginning.

THIRD REVOLUTIONARY: It's the squaring of the circle.

FIRST MAN: Only youth has enough energy and enthusiasm for this.

OLD WOMAN: Young people are more aware than we are.

OLD MAN: The experience of age.

PROPRIETOR: Young people are asses.

FIRST MAN: Old people are asses.

SECOND MAN: There are young asses and old asses; when you're an ass, it's for life.

THIRD REVOLUTIONARY: We'll never sit back and take it again.

WAITRESS: We can't take it anymore, subways, work, kids . . .

WOMAN REVOLUTIONARY (*looking mean and gnashing her teeth*): Revolution for the pleasure of it.

The customers are almost all transformed by this time. We keep their former names for the sake of convenience.

OLD WOMAN: For the pleasure of it.

OLD MAN: Ah yes, for the pleasure.

WAITRESS (*the others have changed clothes and character except the* WAITRESS, *the* CHARACTER, *and the* PROPRIETOR): Revolution for pleasure!

FIRST MAN (*taking out a dagger*): For the pleasure.

SECOND MAN: For the pleasure.

OLD WOMAN, OLD MAN, THIRD REVOLUTIONARY, WAITRESS, FIRST MAN, SECOND MAN, PROPRIETOR, WOMAN REVOLUTIONARY (*one after the other*): Pleasure, pleasure, pleasure.

THIRD REVOLUTIONARY: Good times, you understand? We're going to live in good times. Happiness is in sight. Happiness for forever, happiness for all forever!

They all raise their rifles and guns in agreement. They remain a moment longer with their arms in the air.

THIRD REVOLUTIONARY: Well, all that made me hungry; in fact, I'm starving.

PROPRIETOR: I invite you all to lunch.

THIRD REVOLUTIONARY: I would like to accept, but my wife is waiting at home for me. I don't want her to start worrying. Besides, I've got to rest up a little, at three I've got to be back at my station. However, if you'd like to treat us to a drink before we go, I won't say no . . . and a couple of sandwiches.

The PROPRIETOR *swiftly pours the drinks. They drink.*

Down with the exploitation of man by men!

ALL (*they raise their glasses and shout*): Down with the pigs!

WOMAN REVOLUTIONARY: We'll make soup out of the pigs' ears, eh?

THIRD REVOLUTIONARY (*to the* WAITRESS): Step on it, lady. Hurry it up with those sandwiches. You've got to learn to shape up now, you slut. Things are gonna be different from now on.

WOMAN REVOLUTIONARY: Everything's changed, nothing's the way it was.

ALL (*one after the other*): Nothing's the way it was.

WAITRESS (*to the* THIRD REVOLUTIONARY): I'm doing my best. You're not very polite, you know.

FIRST MAN: Polite, she says.

SECOND MAN: Oh polite, that's right.

OLD WOMAN: Polite is a middle-class word.

THIRD REVOLUTIONARY (*to the* WAITRESS *and the* PROPRIE-TOR): You're both in business. You're exploiters just like the others.

WAITRESS: I'm a worker, that's what I am. I earn my living with the sweat of my brow. All you do is talk.

THIRD REVOLUTIONARY: Bitch!

WAITRESS: Oh!

CHARACTER (*getting up from his table*): Sir, have you no shame?

THIRD REVOLUTIONARY: You lousy middle-class worm!

He strikes the CHARACTER *and sends him flying back to his chair.*

WOMAN REVOLUTIONARY: Good work.

PROPRIETOR: Look here, he's my customer.

The WAITRESS *slaps the* THIRD REVOLUTIONARY *hard across the face twice. He falls to the floor, gets up, feels his jaw. Laughter breaks out, then everyone except the* WAITRESS *and the* PROPRIETOR *turn on the* CHARACTER *aggressively.*

ALL: You rat!

The THIRD REVOLUTIONARY *stays put, shaking his fist at the* CHARACTER. *The* WAITRESS *goes toward the* CHARACTER, *takes a handkerchief out of the* CHARACTER'*s pocket and wipes his bloody face.*

WAITRESS: This sort of thing is not for you.

We hear the noise become louder outside the restaurant. The fight has reached them.

CHARACTER (*gets up, keeps the handkerchief to his face*): The fighting has reached us, we're caught.

WAITRESS: Yes, it's reached us, but calm down, don't get upset.

OLD MAN: It's a free-for-all out there.

WOMAN REVOLUTIONARY: It's a holiday.

We hear machine-guns rattling, screams. We see people running with guns and flags.

WOMAN REVOLUTIONARY: It's come closer, it's right here in the neighborhood. Let's go, let's help it, let's see the explosions, the blood, the bodies!

She unfurls a flag.

OLD WOMAN: Long live the flag!

WOMAN REVOLUTIONARY: Let's get out there and be real men!

OLD MAN: It's my recurrent dream. It's like in '77.

OLD WOMAN: Long live murder!

FIRST MAN: Kill for France.

SECOND MAN: The hour of justice has arrived.

PROPRIETOR: Hour of justice.

WOMAN REVOLUTIONARY: Let's get out of here, what're we doing here?

FIRST MAN: The revolution's going on, outside in the street.

SECOND MAN: And we're still here.

WOMAN REVOLUTIONARY: Let's get out of here.

THIRD REVOLUTIONARY: I'll leave with you, but I'll have to go home to my wife for a half hour, just the time to have lunch, and I'll meet up with you after that.

WOMAN REVOLUTIONARY: Into the street!

The WAITRESS and the PROPRIETOR have become their former selves. The others retain their new identities and become very excited at the call to arms. Outside we still see silhouettes of rebels, civilians, and cops, running about.

OUTSIDE VOICES: Down with the pigs.

In the meantime, the CHARACTER *is drinking his brandy, holding his black eye with his handkerchief.*

PROPRIETOR: You can't leave until you've paid the bill.

WAITRESS: Yeah, the bill, the check.

THIRD REVOLUTIONARY: That's all your kind thinks about . . . money.

He takes bills out of his pocket and waves them.

Here's your dirty money.

WOMAN REVOLUTIONARY: Keep your money for the cause.

FIRST MAN: They're rotten capitalists like the rest.

OLD WOMAN: Don't pay them.

OLD MAN: Yes, sign an IOU instead.

SECOND MAN: Yeah, you can go to the Central Committee for your money.

WOMAN REVOLUTIONARY: Don't bother. Kiss my ass instead.

Noise mounts outside.

THIRD REVOLUTIONARY: To the front, citizens!

OLD WOMAN: Get our flag ready.

SECOND MAN: Let's get over to the town square.

FIRST MAN: Let's occupy the city hall and put the mayor in jail.

SECOND MAN: And his assistants, too.

WOMAN REVOLUTIONARY: And the municipal counselors.

PROPRIETOR: They're family men like everyone else.

WAITRESS: They have wives, too.

WOMAN REVOLUTIONARY: What do we care? Get ready, men!

THIRD REVOLUTIONARY: We'll get them all.

OLD WOMAN: They'll beg for mercy.

OLD MAN: Down with fascism!

WOMAN REVOLUTIONARY: Everyone close in behind me.

The THIRD REVOLUTIONARY, *the* OLD WOMAN, OLD MAN, FIRST MAN, SECOND MAN *all get behind as ordered; they softly sing a kind of revolutionary anthem in a kind of jibberish. We make out certain words:* "liberty," "we shall overcome," "to the death."

They cry "hurray" and rush out as the noise mounts thunderously outside. As they exit they knock over chairs, break plates and glasses, grab bottles to take along with them.

CHARACTER (*has gotten up during all this, steps aside to let the mob get by, remains standing after their departure, undecided*): Should I uh . . . should I do something . . . can I help in some way?

THIRD REVOLUTIONARY (*as he leaves*): You good-for-nothing parasite!

OLD MAN: It was like this in Brazil.

THE OTHERS (*as they leave*): Hurray! Down with everything!

They exit at last. The PROPRIETOR *and the* WAITRESS *look at the mess.*

PROPRIETOR: Goddamn!

WAITRESS: Shit!

CHARACTER: Is there anything I can do?

PROPRIETOR: Like what?

CHARACTER: I don't know, help clean up . . . ?

WAITRESS: We'll manage, you just sit down and relax.

CHARACTER: Could I have another brandy, please?

WAITRESS (*cleaning up with the* PROPRIETOR): I'll bring it right away.

SCENE XI

The restaurant.

The PROPRIETOR, *the* WAITRESS/AGNES.

PROPRIETOR: I've already been in a revolution. I could have led this one easily.

WAITRESS: You're too tired for that sort of thing and, what's more, you're too old.

PROPRIETOR: The trouble is that they're not really revolutionaries . . . what they are is reactionaries.

WAITRESS: And their enemies, what're they?

PROPRIETOR: They're reactionaries too. One side's paid by whites, the other by blacks, but both sides are reactionaries.

WAITRESS: They all looked yellow to me.

PROPRIETOR: Don't be a racist.

WAITRESS: Well I am and I admit it. I'm not an anti-racist . . . I'm for all races.

SCENE XII

The restaurant.

The PROPRIETOR, *the* WAITRESS/AGNES, *and the* CHARAC-
TER. *A* WOMAN *runs in, frightened. She's followed shortly
by a* MOTHER *and a* YOUNG MAN, *her wounded son, later by
two* POLICEMEN *and a* MAN.

MOTHER: Oh please, my son's hurt, help him, in God's
name.

A YOUNG MAN *staggers in, he's wounded, with a bandage around his head. The* PROPRIETOR *and the* WAITRESS

rush toward him to keep him from collapsing. They ease him to the floor.

MOTHER: I told him to be careful, I knew something would happen.

WOMAN: How careful can one be? Life is so short.

PROPRIETOR: She's the widow who lives up the street. Her husband died last year. Young people today don't know what danger is.

MOTHER: My poor baby, my baby.

WOMAN: I've never seen anything like this. What kind of a world are we living in? We had such a nice, quiet neighborhood.

MOTHER (*bending over her son*): What have they done to him? He was so gentle, so kind.

WOMAN: We worked all our lives, we retire, we feel we've earned the right to a little peace and quiet. There's no peace anywhere.

PROPRIETOR: That's life . . . in the end, we die. (*To the* MOTHER.) He might pull through.

WOMAN: Yes, young people have amazing powers of recuperation.

WAITRESS: He's just fainted.

WOMAN: You see, he's still moving.

PROPRIETOR: Yes, he's still moving . . . sort of jerking.

WAITRESS: Don't crowd him like that, give him some air.

PROPRIETOR: Is he really breathing?

WOMAN: His legs are shaking . . . like a frog's.

MOTHER: A doctor, please call a doctor.

WAITRESS: We should call a hospital so they can come for him in an ambulance.

PROPRIETOR: Ambulances can't get around in this mess. There are roadblocks all over.

WAITRESS: That's right, there're traffic jams everywhere. Nothing's moving.

WOMAN (*to* MOTHER): It's his own fault. He shouldn't have gotten mixed up in this.

PROPRIETOR: Who should, then?

MOTHER: I told you, darling, I told you, didn't I? Your friends got you into this. I told you not to go with them.

PROPRIETOR: Who were his friends?

WOMAN: The delinquents who hung around the corner drug stores . . . René and Michel.

PROPRIETOR: Where are they now?

WOMAN: Out making revolutions. Anything but get a decent job.

PROPRIETOR: When I was young I did the same thing. But I didn't get hurt at it.

MOTHER: René and Michel are dead, too.

WOMAN: Them too? There won't be any young people left.

WAITRESS: He wanted to follow his friends to the death.

WOMAN: That's loyalty.

MOTHER: Please call someone, phone for help.

PROPRIETOR (*to* WAITRESS): Try phoning, go ahead. Maybe an ambulance can get through.

WAITRESS: I'll try.

She goes to telephone and starts dialing.

PROPRIETOR: Let's see if we can get him to drink some brandy. That might bring him to.

The PROPRIETOR *and the* WOMAN *try to pry the boy's lips open to get him to drink.*

WAITRESS: I can't get a line, the wires seem to be cut.

MOTHER: I'm going to try to carry him home. Help me, please. I live right up the street. I'll stretch him out on his bed, his childhood bed. I'll call our family doctor. He's saved his life twice already. He won't refuse to come.

WAITRESS: It's true she lives close by.

Two POLICEMEN *enter with a* MAN.

FIRST POLICEMAN: What's going on here?

SECOND POLICEMAN: Get moving, everyone.

PROPRIETOR: This is my restaurant.

SECOND POLICEMAN: Shut up, you.

MOTHER: Please help him, officer. Take him to a hospital.

FIRST POLICEMAN: Another revolutionary.

SECOND POLICEMAN: Get moving, I said.

FIRST POLICEMAN: How did it happen?

PROPRIETOR: We don't know. He came in and collapsed. And there he is in a pool of blood.

FIRST POLICEMAN: You're sure it's his blood.

MOTHER: It wasn't his fault, officer. He was so kind, so gentle. He let them talk him into it. He could never say no.

WOMAN: It's never anybody's fault. That's what they all say. When he was little, he was already shooting at my chickens with his BB gun.

FIRST POLICEMAN: You keep quiet, lady.

SECOND POLICEMAN: There's nothing we can do for him, it's too late. Can't you see he's dying? He's having convulsions.

FIRST POLICEMAN: Not any more, he isn't. He's already dead.

MOTHER: Don't say that! My little boy, my boy. How he loved his wooden horses.

FIRST POLICEMAN (*to the* MOTHER): Who are you?

WAITRESS: Can't you see it's his mother?

FIRST POLICEMAN: I'm asking who she is, what her name is.

SECOND POLICEMAN (*to* MOTHER): Your papers! (*To others.*) That goes for the rest of you, too.

They all take out their identification papers.

PROPRIETOR: I'm the owner of this place.

WAITRESS: I work here as a waitress.

FIRST POLICEMAN (*to the* CHARACTER): And you, what're you doing all by yourself over there?

WAITRESS: He's a customer.

FIRST POLICEMAN: A customer is he?

SECOND POLICEMAN: What's he doing over there, your customer?

WAITRESS: He comes here for lunch every day.

FIRST POLICEMAN (*to the* CHARACTER): Your papers?

SECOND POLICEMAN: When the fighting was going on, what were you doing?

FIRST POLICEMAN: He was right along with them, I'll bet.

WAITRESS: He's completely out of it.

PROPRIETOR: I'll vouch for that, he's a real dummy.

FIRST POLICEMAN: Nobody asked your opinion. Do you rent rooms here?

PROPRIETOR: Not any more.

WAITRESS (*to* POLICEMEN): Go look for yourselves. The beds are gone.

MOTHER (*to* POLICEMEN): Take him to a hospital, please. He's losing so much blood.

SECOND POLICEMAN: She won't get it through her head, he's lost *all* his blood.

MOTHER: It's not true . . . he's going to be all right.

WOMAN: He's dead, madame, he's dead. Isn't that a shame, a nice quiet neighborhood like this. Retired, decent people we were . . . then the revolution came and did this.

PROPRIETOR: They busted my place up.

FIRST POLICEMAN: We'll take him to the morgue.

SECOND POLICEMAN: We'll get him out of your way.

MOTHER: Don't take him away from me, no!

FIRST POLICEMAN: (*to* MOTHER): You're a suspect, too, lady.

WAITRESS: Why, what did she do?

SECOND POLICEMAN: Where do you get off, asking questions?

FIRST POLICEMAN: And the rest of you, watch out, or we'll take you all in.

PROPRIETOR: Won't you boys have a drink before you go?

WAITRESS: They broke everything when they left, we haven't got a bottle in the place.

FIRST POLICEMAN: Then why offer us a drink? Are you being smart or something?

PROPRIETOR: No, no, look . . . I have a bottle of white wine still unbroken.

FIRST POLICEMAN: There, you see, when there's a will, there's a way.

The PROPRIETOR *serves them drinks which they knock back at once. To do this, they've gone over to the bar, leaving the* YOUNG MAN.

MOTHER: You should be taking care of my son.

SECOND POLICEMAN: She's a pain, that one. We'll take care of him AND you, don't worry.

WOMAN: She's distressed, officer, it's only normal.

The two POLICEMEN *grab the* YOUNG MAN's *arms and drag him out.*

SECOND POLICEMAN (*to* MOTHER): And you, follow us.

MOTHER: Don't take him away from me, please.

FIRST POLICEMAN (*to* PROPRIETOR): You take that woman and shove her into the police van (*meaning* MOTHER).

The PROPRIETOR *does exactly that . . . grabs the* MOTHER *and pulls her out.*

WOMAN: I'm going home.

WAITRESS: Be careful. They're still shooting out there.

WOMAN: I have to get home to feed my cat.

She exits also. We hear machine-guns rattling in the distance. Then shots ring out just outside the door. The PROPRIETOR *runs in. We hear* MOTHER *and* WOMAN *scream.*

PROPRIETOR: They were all killed outside the door.

WAITRESS (*after the sound of an explosion close by*): The ambulance just exploded and so did the black maria with the cops in it.

PROPRIETOR: I told them they should stay.

Bullets whistle and some come through the windows of the restaurant. A bottle is caught by one.

PROPRIETOR: They're determined to get every last one of my bottles.

WAITRESS: We might as well be outside right now, all the windows are broken. Look at them marching and singing out there.

We hear and see the marchers outside the window.

WAITRESS (*to the* CHARACTER): Look, a bullet went right through your hat while it was on the rack.

PROPRIETOR: Let's get the iron shutter down right away, hurry, there's no time to lose.

The PROPRIETOR *and the* WAITRESS *turn the handles to the iron shutter. The* CHARACTER *makes a gesture indicating he is trying to help.*

WAITRESS (*to the* CHARACTER): Don't bother, drink your brandy.

The CHARACTER *goes back and sits down. The other two get the shutter down at last.*

WAITRESS: Finally, wow.

PROPRIETOR: Now we're safe at last. Let them blast themselves to pieces out there. They broke every one of my bottles, the rats.

CHARACTER: There's no more brandy?

PROPRIETOR: I'll go down to the cellar and get some. I've kept a stock down there ever since the last revolution.

CHARACTER: Which one? The one in '40?

PROPRIETOR: No, the one in '32. It was a better year anyway, older, you know. I'm going. (*To* WAITRESS.) There's bread and sliced ham behind the counter.

He disappears down trap.

WAITRESS: Does it still hurt? Don't worry, it's not serious. Let me look at it. What a whopper you caught there. But your eye wasn't hurt. Only around the outside. I'll fix your bandage. You wanted to protect me. That was sweet of you. Well, are you aware of reality now? When it hurts, it's really real, isn't it? You're not dreaming now are you? You're sure you're awake, right?

CHARACTER: I'm not sure.

WAITRESS: Hey, you wouldn't be a little crazy, would you? That's what I like about you, now that I think of it. You must be very unhappy.

The CHARACTER *shrugs his shoulders, indicating negative.*

But you're not really happy either, are you?

He moans and shrugs, again indicating negative.

So you're neither happy nor unhappy? I think that's worse than being outright unhappy. Do I sound like I'm speaking nonsense? Anyway, I think you're nice.

He shrugs again.

Don't you think someone can find you nice? Well, they can.

He remains silent.

You don't have to think about that, or answer it. You look all surprised. I'll bring you some ham and bread. Would you like that?

He points to his empty glass.

ANOTHER brandy? That's too much. Well, just one more then, but it's the last.

She goes for his brandy, brings it to him; he drinks it down. We hear the PROPRIETOR coming up from the cellar. He's singing.

WAITRESS: Listen to him! There's another one who loves to drink. (*To the* CHARACTER.) I really would like to help you. I once knew someone who was like you. He wasn't sick, there wasn't anything wrong with him. In fact he had a lot of things going for him. Well, would you believe he committed suicide? You don't have any ideas about committing suicide do you?

He shrugs his shoulders.

Has anyone ever loved you?

CHARACTER: My mother.

WAITRESS: Of course, but since then? Do you know what it is to be loved? You don't seem as though you do. Am I right? It happens that at the moment I'm free, available. If you'd like . . . but you have to want it, really want it. I'll teach you how to live every moment, I'll teach you to be happy. Don't bulge your eyes like that. I'm not talking through my hat. I can't live without a guy. No woman should live without a man. I'll hold your hand and lead our way. Let yourself go. Follow me.

We keep hearing the strident singing of the PROPRIETOR *going through his choice bottles. Outside, the occasional rat-tat-tat of a machine-gun.*

Oh, that man, the Boss. Well at least he's not a melancholy type. He just doesn't give a damn. Do you hear, the fighting's calming down. We'll be able to leave soon. I don't know why you make me feel so sorry for you. I like that in you, I guess. You're different from the others. Don't you ever say anything? Hasn't anything I've said made an impression on you? I repeat, I'm available at the moment. I can see that you're alone too. The stones will move out from in front of our path, the route will be smooth. My hands are a little rough, the skin's not as soft as it used to be. Well, that's normal. I work for a living, hands in the water all day long doing dishes. But the skin on my body is very smooth. I have pretty eyes, look! I'm still young, and you're not old either. I was never really unhappy. I have a lucky star up there somewhere. It will guide both of us. I have a nice bustline, my legs are well shaped, my eyes are expressive . . . I've been told that, and I know it's true. I'll teach you, everything, everything. You got off to a wrong start, a wrong turn somewhere. With me you'll get back on the right road. (*She caresses his hand. He pulls it away.*) What are you afraid of? You wanted to protect me, I'll never forget that. I don't think you could protect yourself if you tried. Isn't that right? Don't bother answering, your silence is answer enough and so is your look. I don't know what's come over me, but with you I'm not like with the others. With you I feel different. You don't even dare to kiss me and yet I feel that what I've told you makes you feel good. Have you ever loved anyone besides your mother? Has anyone ever loved you? No? No one? Because you're shy, because you don't know how to express yourself, because you have no confidence in yourself? I'll give you confidence in yourself. People kill each other, they tear each other to pieces, they're jealous of each other, they exploit each other. That takes up all their time and space. But we'll have both time and space. Just enough. It's not selfish of us, we'll set an example for the others. There has to be a tiny little beginning of love somewhere, of confidence. They'll see us. They'll be surprised and finally they'll follow us. Instead of troops marching and crying out for murder, there'll be long lines of couples who love each other. Endless lines of couples strolling along tree-lined paths where rose bushes grow without thorns.

We hear the PROPRIETOR *again singing his wine song. From the outside we hear curses: Bastard, Pigs, We'll get 'em, No pity for the exploiters, etc.*

Don't be afraid, don't be upset, those cries are far away. Wait a little while.

She goes to the window and raises the iron shutter up halfway.

They're gone. They've left the town square.

The PROPRIETOR *finally comes up carrying bottles.*

PROPRIETOR: Is your customer still here?

WAITRESS: He couldn't leave, we had the iron shutter down.

PROPRIETOR: Well, don't raise it yet. Leave it the way it is. What's happening outside?

He goes over to the window on all fours and peers out.

One, two, three, four, five, six, seven, eight. Eight bodies out there on the sidewalk.

WAITRESS: They may only be wounded or dying.

PROPRIETOR: Two policemen among them. Serves them right! They should have kept out of it.

WAITRESS: It's their business, isn't it?

PROPRIETOR: They could have chosen another business. When people want to wipe each other out, the crime is to try and stop them. In the meantime, they broke up everything in my place and that's a crime too.

WAITRESS (*to the* CHARACTER): Come on, let's go. We can get through now, the wounded and dying aren't dangerous. There are blood puddles in the streets, but don't worry, you won't get your shoes dirty, I'll guide you. Where there is blood today, there'll be flowers tomorrow.

PROPRIETOR: If my customers kill each other, what'll I do with my stock?

WAITRESS: Come on!

She goes up to the CHARACTER *and kisses him.*

Come, take me away to your house. I know the way already. Come, come. (*She takes his hand.*) Come my love, my darling.

PROPRIETOR: I didn't say you could leave. You've got to clean this mess up.

WAITRESS: Bend down to get under the iron shutter.

The CHARACTER *obeys, he and the* WAITRESS *are on all fours. They crawl right up to the doorway and suddenly he gets up.*

CHARACTER (*to* PROPRIETOR): I haven't paid my bill.

WAITRESS: Don't worry about it, money's not worth anything any more. There's still a civil war going on, there's inflation. Get down and let's get out of here. Hurry!

They exit.

PROPRIETOR: I had customers, they've massacred them. They're satisfied now, dead on the sidewalks with their guts hanging out. I had a regular daily customer. She just took him away. Whatever came over her? (*He goes over to lower the iron shutter again.*) That's strange they haven't cut off the electricity. (*He looks around at the broken bottles, overturned tables and chairs.*) Good thing I carry an insurance policy. Everything is allowed for: fire, flood, war, and revolutions. (*He starts to straighten things out, picks up chairs, tables. New noises are heard outside.*) There they go again. They may make it after all this time. Who knows?

SCENE XIII

The CHARACTER's *apartment.*

The CONCIERGE, *a* YOUNG MAN *with a shoulder-strap rifle,
the* WOMAN WITH THE DOG.

YOUNG MAN: Madame Guardian, here's my key.

CONCIERGE: All right, I'll keep it for you. Where are you
going with that rifle? To fight a revolution? I thought
that was all over?

YOUNG MAN: Don't worry, it'll start up again, right here in
fact, in front of your very windows.

The WOMAN WITH THE DOG *enters.*

WOMAN WITH DOG: Madame Guardian, here's my key. I'm off to the revolution.

CONCIERGE: Your husband has already been killed.

WOMAN WITH DOG: Exactly; it's to replace him that I'm going.

CONCIERGE: All right, but let me clean up at least; the new tenant should be arriving.

WOMAN WITH DOG: Where is the maid you hired, the dumb one?

CONCIERGE: She was killed.

YOUNG MAN: You see, everyone's going to the revolution.

CONCIERGE: She wasn't at the revolution. She was out shopping. They told her to stop and show her identification. I don't know who asked her, the rebels or the police. She didn't answer them because she couldn't talk, and they shot her.

WOMAN WITH DOG: Still, one should participate in a revolution.

CONCIERGE: I've got too much work to do. I've got this whole house to take care of!

YOUNG MAN: We'll be back when we've overthrown the establishment.

CONCIERGE: You make revolutions because there are no more metaphysical theories to hang on to. You don't realize it, but it's the existential condition which is in bad shape. The social and economic conditions are not too bad, all things considered. They're not great, I'll admit that. However, we have seen that almost all societies are rotten. There is no "good" society. Tyranny, dictatorship, liberalism, capitalism, all are no good. There is no economy, whether social or liberal, that can resolve the problems of human economic needs. We know this for sure. Just read the papers. They try to hide the truth, but it comes through just the same. There is nothing but genocide and massacres going on all over the world.

YOUNG MAN: Don't get mixed up in that sort of thinking; you don't understand anything about politics.

CONCIERGE (*while sweeping*): You say that because I'm house guardian and housekeeper. That's not very democratic of you.

YOUNG MAN: I'm not for democracy. I'm for the people.

CONCIERGE: The people is me.

WOMAN WITH DOG: You're not the liberated people—you're servile.

YOUNG MAN: You're paid by the ruling class.

CONCIERGE: There're no ruling classes here . . . just retired people.

WOMAN WITH DOG: They have a ruling class mentality.

YOUNG MAN (*to* WOMAN WITH DOG): Are you coming with me, my sweet? First we'll make revolution together and then we'll make love.

WOMAN WITH DOG: Oh yes. After the revolution or before?

YOUNG MAN: During. All the time. Revolution is merely the explosion of my desires.

WOMAN WITH DOG: Marvelous!

YOUNG MAN: All desires.

WOMAN WITH DOG: You're my desire.

YOUNG MAN: Let's go make love. You're not beautiful, but revolution makes you shine. And long live death! (*To* CONCIERGE.) Goodbye, Madame Guardian. I scorn you.

WOMAN WITH DOG: I feel sorry for you. You're a slave.

CONCIERGE: And your social gatherings? Your teas and your cocktail parties? What's to become of them? Are you dropping all that?

WOMAN WITH DOG: I expect to be back every day between five and seven, between attacks.

YOUNG MAN: Whenever possible, dear, I'd rather we lay somewhere together, on grass or pavement, between five and seven.

CONCIERGE (*while sweeping*): You don't know what you want. You can't choose between the desire to live and the desire to die. Eros and Thanatos. Sitting between two chairs.

YOUNG MAN (*to* WOMAN WITH DOG): Let us be off, my pet. Let us hurry. She doesn't know what she's talking about.

CONCIERGE: You don't know what you're doing. You're preparing the apocalypse.

YOUNG MAN: She's talking bullshit.

CONCIERGE: There're two real dangers facing humanity: overpopulation and pollution of the environment.

WOMAN WITH DOG: You talk in clichés.

CONCIERGE: Don't you? Only mine are true and yours are lies.

YOUNG MAN: Bullshit!

CONCIERGE: You kill and at the same time you make children. What an incredible contradiction.

WOMAN WITH DOG: Bullshit!

CONCIERGE: Neither of you is very polite.

WOMAN WITH DOG: Politeness is a middle-class institution.

CONCIERGE: And you, aren't you middle-class . . . and isn't it the middle class who's out making this revolution?

WOMAN WITH DOG: I am no longer middle-class. As a matter of fact, I'm a widow. My husband died during an attack. And now I have a proletariat lover.

YOUNG MAN (*to* WOMAN WITH DOG): You hear? The machine-guns have quieted down. We can't let them stop altogether. Let's go do our part.

They kiss and they exit.

CONCIERGE: What if it did stop and everything got worked out? You wouldn't like that at all, would you? You don't want it to stop and work out at all.

YOUNG MAN (*voice off*): Things would be too boring. What would we do without the revolution?

CONCIERGE: What's the point of trying to reason with them?
Reason has nothing to do with this.

Sound of gunfire from outside.

Is my poor tenant going to be able to come in? Things
are getting bad again. Now it's right here on our street.
Before it was in the square. I'm going to soundproof this
place. Now, where are those mattresses I had? Mattresses,
mattresses. If they do get back, at least they'll have some
peace and quiet. (*She finds the mattresses and stands
them up against the windows which face the street.*)
The era of revolutions is over, don't they know that? All
government regimes are bad, but they're all very much
installed. Playing politics is over. Revolution is just an
obsession, an obsessive fixation, a no-no. They still make
revolutions, but they don't serve any purpose. It's time
for technology and industrialization to take over. But they
won't inspire passions to rise. What would they do without their passions? They'd get bored, as they say. Two
centuries of revolutions to end up with dictatorships and
tyranny. Have revolutions ever set off anything good?
Technology hasn't either, for that matter. It has covered
our planet with wastes. Our planet has become a waste
receptacle. In fifty years there will be thirty billion people on earth. That's the problem. That's the real problem.
Can we reverse the situation? There's no way. We're
slipping right down into disaster and we can't stop it. It's
the creator's fault. He said, "Love one another," but it's
not possible. The truth is, "Eat one another." Everything
is in conflict. Women, men, animals, insects, plants . . .
we're all obliged to eat each other. Our nourishment
comes from no other source. We live in a closed-circuit

economy. Oh, if only we didn't have to eat. The horror is that when we breathe, we kill, when we move a little bit, we massacre millions of microscopic creatures. If only there were no hotheads. We kill to dress ourselves, we kill trees to have a roof, we kill plants to make textiles. What a glory hole this cosmos of ours is. We must find food where we are. So we eat ourselves and each other. Yes, maybe that's right. It's the existentialist condition which is bad, very bad. (*She takes up her broom again; she speaks while gesturing with it.*) The existential condition creates a bad society, a bad economy, a bad political situation. Every now and then, thank heaven, the police act up and there's repression. With police and repression we'd devour each other with even more speed. In our country, repression is resigning and the polite are revolting too. Police explode with desire too, I suppose. I'm for freedom. I'm not sure I'm still for freedom for the individual. Men are mad. They've got to be held in check. In totalitarian countries they have some sense of order at least. It's depressive, but there's order. Nobody is allowed to move. They devour each other less. They can only devour within the framework of the freedom allowed, which is limited. It's decidedly less. Is that better? (*She sweeps with agitation.*) Well, I don't care any more. Let them blow themselves up. Let them massacre themselves. Let things rip, explode, burn up and then that's that. The human adventure has lasted long enough. Let it be over with and not worry us any longer. The creator put his foot in it with this one. (*She sweeps on.*)

SCENE XIV

The CHARACTER'S *apartment.*

The CONCIERGE, *the* CHARACTER, *the* WAITRESS/AGNES.

The CHARACTER *and the* WAITRESS *enter.*

CONCIERGE: Ah, there you are! (*Upon noticing the* WAIT-
RESS.) Uh, how do you do?

WAITRESS: I'm your tenant's girlfriend. I might even be his
fiancée. In any case, I live with him.

CONCIERGE: Congratulations, sir. That's very nice. It's never
a good idea to live alone. It's much worse than living in

couples or more. I was afraid you wouldn't be able to come home. What a fight we had right here on our street.

WAITRESS: Who is doing all the fighting?

CONCIERGE: Always the same ones, I mean it's the same political party. Behind the barricades at the end of the street, there's the green flag with a red square in the center. At the other end of the street, there's the same flag. But you two will be all right. I've blocked up the windows with mattresses. You can barely hear the noises outside. I used everything I could find including the mattresses—cushions, sand bags, everything. And I've got some food stored away in the cellar which we can live on till things calm down. Good night, sir. Good night, miss.

WAITRESS: It's nice in your house. It feels like I'm on vacation. It's not the beach of course, but it's nice anyway. Do you know my name? It's Agnes. What a time we had getting home, eh? They even took a shot at the white handkerchief you were waving. Look, it's got a hole in it. But you weren't hurt, there's at least that. There's another hole in your hat. That makes two. Kiss me. Do you remember my name? Agnes. Come sit down in this armchair. I'll sit down beside you, at your feet.

The CHARACTER *sits down, then gets up.*

Where are you going? Why are you going toward that window? Don't open that up. Don't open it, I said. Why do you want to open it? What are you doing?

The CHARACTER *goes toward the right-hand corner where a rifle is standing, the one the* YOUNG MAN *left behind.*

Leave that rifle alone, you don't even know how to use it.

The CHARACTER *examines the rifle carefully. By accident he pulls the trigger. A shot rings out.*

For God's sake, you could have killed me.

The CHARACTER *seems frightened by the shot.*

It's a good thing you were pointing toward the mattress. If I had been standing there, do you realize what would have happened?

He continues to wander around the room with the rifle over his shoulder.

You want to fight? With who?

He shrugs his shoulders.

You don't even know. Aren't you afraid?

He shakes his head no.

Are you brave?

He shakes his head no.

Not afraid and not brave either.

He goes toward the door.

Come on, stay here.

He stops.

Go put that rifle away.

He remains standing in place in the middle of the stage. We hear a couple of distant shots outside.

You hear? They're answering you. No, it's not an echo. A rifle shot is like the howling of a dog. One starts and another replies. Why don't you get me an orange drink instead? That trip we just made getting here, dodging bullets and rebels, made me thirsty. I'm hot, too. It's nice here.

She lies down on the sofa, stretches out.

CHARACTER: Something?

WAITRESS: What something?

CHARACTER: Something I should be doing, I guess.

WAITRESS: For who, for what?

CHARACTER (*shrugging his shoulders*): Oh, that's difficult to know.

WAITRESS: You can see that it exists just the same, that's for real.

CHARACTER: It's strange . . . existence is so bloody.

WAITRESS: But I exist too, isn't that right? Don't you feel that? Aren't I real?

CHARACTER: I think so. I mean, yes, of course, yes.

WAITRESS: And you, do you exist?

CHARACTER (*after a few moments of thought*): Uh yes, I am.

WAITRESS: You're sure that you ARE, but you're not sure you exist.

CHARACTER: Yes, I am.

WAITRESS: Then others exist also. We exist through the others, in fact.

CHARACTER: Oh?

The CHARACTER *goes to the phone, picks up the receiver, and dials a number.*

WAITRESS: What are you doing, darling?

CHARACTER: I have a friend who's a philosopher. He'll explain it to me.

He waits expectantly; there's no reply.

WAITRESS: The telephone lines were cut by the rebels. Hang up.

He hangs up.

WAITRESS: Go put your rifle away.

He props the rifle in a corner.

WAITRESS: Come sit down in the armchair. C'mon, do it.

He goes over and sits in the armchair. Pauses.

CHARACTER: Still, you know, we should really . . . uh . . .

WAITRESS: We should do something, yes I know, you said that. Why? I'm asking you, why?

He shrugs his shoulders.

Do you have any ambitions? You have demands to make of society or something you feel you have to assert? Do you have needs which are ungratified, like the others out there? You detest something special or something general in some vague way? Do you love someone? You love no one, right? That is, you just love me.

He shakes his head yes.

Is that true? Say it then, darling.

He shakes his head yes again.

Oh I'm so happy. You see, you do know what you want.

He shakes his head yes again.

Well then, how about that orange drink? You know where the bottle of orangeade is? Come to think of it, I'd rather have a cup of tea. I'll go make us a pot of tea. How good it feels, just the two of us, safe and sound and cozy here.

The WAITRESS, *that is,* AGNES, *exits to make the tea. We hear her humming from the wings. The* CHARACTER *stays in his armchair for a long moment. Finally* AGNES *reappears with the tea and serves it. They both drink.*

AGNES: They won't set the house on fire. It's strange how they changed. They were the same customers and yet they'd changed into different people.

CHARACTER: It was as though they were in transparent coffins.

AGNES: Maybe you were just sleepwalking.

CHARACTER: In any case, they were fussing away a lot like a bunch of half-crazed schemers. You asked me what I want? I would like to change the place of the sun.

AGNES: You hear? They're still shooting. Haven't stopped. That's three months it's been going on. We'll take a trip on a beautiful white boat, between sky and sea. Long days on the boat, on the bow of the boat, in the sun. We'll be all tanned. The white boat, the blue sky, and water, and then two handsome crewmen, two captains in white uniforms in the southern seas. It rains a lot on the equator. When we pass the equator while it rains, we'll take shelter under the parasols and sip cold drinks till the air clears up and the clouds disappear. There'll be a new sky, all washed off, all cleaned, all blue again. As we near the coast, we'll see white rowboats with black natives in them, fishermen, and there'll be gulls flying around and we'll see the land, the new land. We'll debark on the new continent, no one will have seen it or discovered it, not even Christopher Columbus. There'll be trees bearing fruits which no one's ever tasted. It'll be a continent or maybe just islands. No, it'll be a continent, a new continent. We'll plunge into a new continent. There no one will know what war is about. As we approach the city ramparts, the gates will open to us. We'll step inside and stroll around the sunlit streets of a golden city.

We hear the rattle of machine-guns.

They'll offer us huge bouquets of flowers and we won't have enough arms and heads for the bouquets and the crowns.

The CHARACTER *listens unmoved.*

Red flowers, yellow and blue ones. There people live in great houses that look like palaces. They dance and laugh and sing.

A Hell of a Mess

All during AGNES' *daydreaming we hear gunfire, shout-ing, fighting muffled in the distance.*

They make love all day long. All night long. At night huge stars come out, they look so close you could reach out and touch them. At the street corners and vil-lage squares, there are ladders suspended in the sky which we can climb, ladders made of silver. No one uses them because people are so happy where they are in their own land, on earth. It's not the same earth as we have. It's a sweet earth, soft like a huge plush carpet. You're greeted and welcomed because in this country they like foreigners. And you can leave the city by the opposite gates after crossing it. The continent is large. There're hundreds and thousands of other cities, flow-ered cities, happy places, one more joyful than the next. There are many lakes on this continent where the water is soft and transparent and the mountains which surround them are tall and white-capped. And the further you go into this continent, the more beautiful it becomes, more exciting and flowered and surprising. There are lions on the roads, but they're gentle and friendly as the lambs they lead into pastures where the grass never withers. Yes of course it's true, since I find it all in my head. They all love each other and, because they love each other, they never grow old. It's difficult to reach this land. You get there by accident, by luck because of a fluke mistake in navigation. How does one commit that kind of an error in navigation? The officers of the ship know their busi-ness so well, but luckily the younger ones don't and they're lucky enough to lose their way. Then there are the old captains, a little dotty, slightly tipsy, who've forgotten some of the rules. Thank God for them. The boat which lowers its anchor in that port will never raise it again. Or if they do return here, it's because they're sorry for the others who live their dull lives and haven't found the miraculous route yet. They return to tell them, to explain, to take them away too. Most of the time when they return to take back others, they can't find their way back. Then it's too late, they've no strength left because even though back there they stay young, they've gotten older as they make their way back here. Once there, you must forget everything, otherwise you'll never know whether it's true or a dream.

CHARACTER: What color are the eyes of the people there?

AGNES: The color of light.

CHARACTER: What is the percentage of illiteracy in the cities of that continent?

AGNES: You hear? They're still making that awful noise out there with their rifles and machine-guns. You can hear them if you pay attention. I had an uncle who was in charge of running a train station. I used to go with him and sleep in my cousin's room. After a while we'd stop hearing the trains coming and going any more. Or when we would hear them, the noise would just lull us to sleep.

The CONCIERGE *enters.*

CONCIERGE: It's dinner time. I brought it up for you, piping hot.

The CONCIERGE *puts down the food and leaves.*

AGNES: How time passes. It must be a month that I'm here. Are you happy to be with me?

The CHARACTER *remains silent.*

When we can start going out again, we'll visit the desert too. There are no limits to what we can do. There are abandoned cities there. There are cities buried so deep you have to climb down to visit them. There are others which are just at the surface of the earth and shine in the sunlight. Why were they abandoned? I wonder. Because the people there wanted to build other cities, further away but still in the desert. In the abandoned cities there are streets still intact, houses with furniture and utensils intact. Even telephones and preserved food in some cases. It was done deliberately to receive visitors. There are long stretches of golden sand and others of red earth. There's a red sun and a red moon, too.

CHARACTER: I don't hear the guns anymore. You think it's over?

AGNES: What difference does it make to you? I guess it's not normal to live the way we live, holed up in a place with mattresses hiding the windows where we're hanging on for as long as the electricity holds out or the water holds out. It's a love nest, that's what it is. There are thousands, hundreds of thousands of people like us in the world. You'll go out later when you're stronger. We'll go out together. You'll live like everyone else, we'll live like all the others, a normal life.

CHARACTER: Normal?

AGNES: Of course, normal. You're going to learn what a normal life is. As a matter of fact, right now we're living a normal life.

CHARACTER: A normal life?

AGNES: Oh, don't be so annoying. Yes, you'll see.

CHARACTER: I'd like to know what's happening outside.

AGNES: Don't make a move. Wait a little longer. Don't move, I told you.

He doesn't listen and goes for his rifle.

CHARACTER: It's not to shoot with. I just want to put out a white flag.

AGNES: They're going to think it's a trick. Take the broom instead. Oh, I've got to explain everything to you, do everything for you. I don't know why I ever got involved with you. I don't know why I love you. Maybe I don't, maybe I'm just sorry for you. Maybe I find you incredible.

During her speech, she has put a white dust cloth at the end of the broomstick. She hands it to the CHARACTER. He takes it, pushes the mattress aside somewhat, and prepares to put the broomstick out the window.

Don't be afraid to break the window, they've been broken for some time. But be careful, for God's sake.

The CHARACTER pushes the broomstick out and we hear a sharp shot at once. He pulls it back in and we see blood splashed on the white cloth.

AGNES: You see, I told you. You never want to listen. Be patient! Why are you so anxious to get outside and see the war?

CHARACTER: I'm not.

AGNES: It's very hard to try and figure you out.

CHARACTER: How come there's blood on the cloth?

AGNES: Because the hole was made by a bullet which killed somebody en route, that's how come. Or maybe the bullet was used a couple of times. It's the blood of others. (*She takes the broomstick, removes the cloth, puts the broomstick in the corner next to the rifle, looks closely at the white cloth.*) That's some hole! A big one with a bloody halo around it. It's the color of fire. I'll mend this and wash it clean.

The CONCIERGE *arrives with other dishes of food.*

CONCIERGE: No, madame, you won't be able to mend this hole and that blood will never come out. Keep it as a souvenir. Oh, you haven't eaten the lunch I brought you? Aren't you hungry? That's because neither of you gets enough exercise.

She takes away the tray with the old dishes and leaves the new one.

CONCIERGE: Well, hope you enjoy it. (*She exits.*)

AGNES: Come on, she's right, let's walk around a little, it'll do you good. Come on, let's go. Oh, there you go lying on the sofa again. (*She takes his hand and pulls him up.*) Walk, One, Two!

He walks, dragging himself around.

Faster!

He walks somewhat faster.

That's not fast enough. Come on. Let's see a jog. Give me your hand.

They jog from stage left to right; they stop, out of breath.

Let's just walk. Look, we're on a path surrounded with rose bushes. Even right over our heads. There's grass under our feet. What a beautiful lawn we're on. Look over there, that lovely white house. Let's walk a little more. How soft the air is. You hear the ripple of water somewhere? And the birds? Now it's all quiet again. And now the stars are out, and the moon. What a beautiful night! Take a deep breath of this wonderful country air.

The CHARACTER *stops for an instant. He listens.*

No, it's not machine-guns any more, nor bombs either. It's the summer thunder in the distance. Did you breathe deeply? Are you hungry now? Let's sit down and eat.

They sit down together.

CHARACTER: I want a brandy.

AGNES: You will not have a brandy now.

CHARACTER: I want a brandy now.

AGNES: You know it's no good for you, it hurts you. There are no doctors left to take care of you. They were all murdered so they wouldn't be able to take care of the rebels.

CHARACTER: I said I want brandy! We've got plenty in reserve. And besides, I'm never hungry when I'm home.
You think they'll reopen the restaurant soon?

AGNES: Oh, I'll bring you your brandy. If I'm not enough
for you . . .

*She brings him brandy, and pours him a drink. He drinks
it in one shot and sits silently.*

AGNES: Well, go on, talk to me about something.

*He remains silent. She gets up, clears away the table,
goes toward the back with the tray at the place where the*
CONCIERGE *enters and exits. The* CONCIERGE *takes it
from her.*

CONCIERGE: Good night, madame, sir. (*She exits.*)

AGNES: Don't you have anything to say to me?

Silence.

You used to talk a lot. You used to actually say a few
words on your own every now and then.

The CHARACTER *silently goes over to the sofa and lies
down on it as* AGNES *watches him.*

AGNES: Don't you want to kiss me? Take me in your arms,
darling.

The CHARACTER *gets up, goes toward* AGNES, *and places
a kiss on her forehead. She tries to take him in her arms.
He breaks away and goes over to the armchair, into which
he settles deeply.*

CHARACTER: It's been so long since we've gotten a newspaper.

AGNES: Tomorrow I'll tell the Concierge to bring us one. They must've started printing some by now. With new sensational headlines, I'm sure. The world is transforming itself, everything's moving, changing. Certainly nothing is the same. It can't be.

CHARACTER (*after a moment of silence*): You think the fighting's still going on in the north suburb or in the center city? I'm sure the center's quiet by now.

AGNES: Maybe. I don't know.

She sits down too, after having tried to put her arms around him. He pulls away, goes to get the brandy, and sits back down in his armchair with the bottle in hand.

CHARACTER: I would really like to go out and see. It used to be so nice, before.

AGNES: What used to be so nice?

CHARACTER: Work. I used to work with Jacques Dupont, no Jean Dupont. Yes, that's right, it was Jean Dupont. It was tiring.

AGNES: Things were better when they were tiring?

He shakes his head yes enthusiastically.

But now that you don't work or do anything, you're tired just the same.

CHARACTER: Yes, but in those days there were Sundays.

AGNES: What did you do on Sundays?

CHARACTER: I'd be bored.

AGNES: Just like now?

CHARACTER: No, it was boring, but better. I'd sit at café terraces, I'd drink beer, and I'd watch the couples passing. And the sidewalks would shine at night under the street lamps. There were puddles in the gutters. Next door to the café there was a movie house.

AGNES: What kind of movies did they show?

CHARACTER: Action movies with guns, and battles, and lovers who'd shoot guns and die.

AGNES: Like the civil war we've just seen and still have around us; it's not over yet. It might even be over for all I know; it's been three months I've been in here with you. You sure you're not confusing the movies with what's been going on here? You're mixing everything up.

CHARACTER: I don't know any more. The usher used to wake me up. I'd go home to my hotel. The bed was never made. There were so many other extraordinary things in those days.

AGNES: When were THOSE DAYS?

CHARACTER: It was . . . I don't remember.

AGNES: Was it yesterday?

CHARACTER: Yes, it was yesterday.

AGNES: Yesterday you were here with me!

CHARACTER: Was I? Then it wasn't yesterday.

AGNES: Was it last month?

CHARACTER: Yes, yes, it was last month.

AGNES: Last month you were still here with me. You stuck out the white flag, remember? It came back in with a hole and blood on it. Look, it's still standing in the corner.

CHARACTER: Then it wasn't last month.

AGNES: It wasn't three months ago either because it's been three months that I've been here with you. We left the restaurant after the fight. We made our way here dodging bullets. Your hat still has the hole a bullet put in it, you know that.

CHARACTER: Well then, it was another day, another evening, another rain. There were streets and there were people. And policemen. And then once I heard church bells, I went toward them and there was a great cathedral and crowds of people. One day, another day, there was a long white path.

AGNES: There are churches everywhere, crowds everywhere. Fights everywhere and funerals too. There are white crosses everywhere and love is everywhere too.

CHARACTER: Oh, well, perhaps.

AGNES: There is love, yes. You have love right next to you. Well, at least I'm fond of you. I'm not sure whether it's fondness or love, but I'm sure that I AM love.

CHARACTER: Oh of course, it's true. There was Lucienne.

AGNES: Lucienne? Who was that?

CHARACTER: It was Lucienne.

AGNES: A mistress of yours?

CHARACTER: Yes.

AGNES: Lucienne was me. You could never have had another mistress with your attitude. With your neurotic personality, with the boredom you give out. You couldn't have had anyone but me. No one else would be crazy enough.

CHARACTER: She was tall.

AGNES: And what else?

CHARACTER: She had eyes which were . . . which were blue-green, yes, a mixture. Not like yours. She was another type of woman. She was blonde, no, she was brunette. Or was she a redhead?

AGNES: She never existed.

CHARACTER: Yes, she did, since she used to spend nights with me.

AGNES: What did she ever see in you? She must've been crazy.

CHARACTER: She was.

AGNES: I'm crazy.

CHARACTER: You are.

AGNES: I'm the one who's crazy? It's you who's crazy, nuts, crackers, unstrung.

CHARACTER: I'm waiting.

AGNES: For what? What're you waiting for? You have everything within your reach. I'm here and you won't touch me and you're afraid. Yes, you seem as though you're afraid. Oh, if only you wanted, if only you'd dare. What are you waiting for?

CHARACTER: I'm waiting for an opening, a crack through which something will come to us. Don't you understand? I feel that no country is my country. I'm waiting for a crack in the wall. Maybe that will cause everything to crumble. There won't be any more walls. No more covers, no more boards on the earth, no more spaces without limit . . . perhaps, perhaps.

AGNES: In the meantime, you shut yourself up and you shut me up with you. And here we are walled in and you put mattresses against the windows, and you put new shutters on top of old shutters, and you add walls to walls that already exist. Do you realize what you're saying?

CHARACTER: No.

AGNES: Oh, you are pitiful. I don't know why I'm fool enough to stay with you. Come on, it's late . . . come on now, let's go to bed, honey.

CHARACTER: Yes, let's sleep. (AGNES *goes over to the light switch.*) No, don't turn it off, please! I'm afraid of the night.

AGNES: I'm sick and tired of this light which has been on day and night for all the months I've been with you. You can't tell whether it's night or day, whether there's sunshine out or stars. Ah, there're paradises on this earth, I swear to you, there are.

She lies down next to him on the sofa after having picked up a blanket.

I'll kiss you goodnight anyway.

He's silent. She kisses him. He doesn't respond. She kisses him again. He reacts the same way, meaning he doesn't. She sighs.

What was Lucienne like?

She falls asleep. A few moments of silence and immobility pass. We hear creaking noises coming from the outside and then other sounds: sledgehammer sounds, but quiet ones, singing, etc. The CHARACTER *gets up cautiously and walks around the room. He looks at all the walls, the furniture as though he were seeing them for the first time. He peeks past one of the mattresses against one window and quickly withdraws. He goes around the room once again, then he goes over to* AGNES, *who remains asleep. He pulls away the blanket and peers down at her in her semi-nude state, looks at her legs, her thighs, touches her lightly so as not to waken her, and his expression suddenly changes from that of curious surprise to that of fright.*

CHARACTER: What a wound, what a deep, bloody wound you carry around with you, you poor creature.

He is suddenly panicked and rushes from one side of the stage to the other. His expression is one of surprise, fear, panic, all at the same time. He guzzles brandy from the bottle. He collapses stage center, after running into and turning over a chair. He sleeps. For a long moment, nothing happens while AGNES *and the* CHARACTER *sleep in their separate places.*

SCENE XV

The CHARACTER'S *apartment.*

The CHARACTER, AGNES, *the* CONCIERGE, *the* PROPRIETOR, *the* MOTHER OF THE CHARACTER, *the* CHARACTER'S SCHOOL TEACHER, JACQUES DUPONT'S SON, AGNES' DAUGHTER, *the* SON OF THE LOVER OF THE WOMAN WITH THE DOG, *the* SON OF THE REVOLUTIONARY WHO PUNCHED THE CHARACTER IN THE NOSE, TWO MEN, *a* WOMAN.

The CONCIERGE *enters. Slowly and seemingly having nothing to do with the entrance of the* CONCIERGE, AGNES *and the* CHARACTER *awake and get up.*

CONCIERGE: Here's your breakfast.

AGNES: Did Lucienne ever exist? What're you staring at me like that for? Do I scare you? Well, so I do, it seems. I can't take your monkey eyes, frightened all the time.

CONCIERGE: You know, it's morning and the weather is lovely out. The fighting is gone now. It's far away from here, in any case. The massacres and the genocides are so far away that we don't even have to think about them any more. It's somebody else's problem now. Those are things which happen to others now.

CHARACTER: I don't want to go out anymore.

CONCIERGE: Every now and then a traveler comes in by plane and he tells us what's going on. Or else there's some mention in the newspaper. Or maybe a word on the radio or television. The printers go to work and there it is—comic strip accounts of everything that has taken place. You see, look. (*She unfolds the images.*) Neighborhood girl is dead on barricades: football hero dies in bullet crossfire; safety patrol is machine-gunned by accident. It's become history already. If you want to know, I was against it. But now I think it was beautiful. It's colorful history, it's . . . legend. When you have children, they'll read all about it in books. Well, when's the wedding for, and when're the children coming? You've been together two years now. Well, anyway, can I take away the mattresses and let the daylight in?

CHARACTER: No.

AGNES: I can't stand it any longer. Everyone would understand and say I'm right.

CONCIERGE: The lady with the dog was killed during the fighting, her dog too. The young man killed her husband. They were in the same political group, but they had personal differences. The White Russian with the cane, he's dead too. The mother of the young man who was hurt, remember her? Well she's still there. Her son died at the hospital long ago. The old lady, the ex-owner here, the one who sold you this apartment, well she used to write me. Then the mails weren't working for a long time and, ever since, she doesn't write any more. And that's it. And then my husband died too. One has to take it all with good will. It's life!

She exits.

CHARACTER: Ever since the revolution is over, the banks work more and better than before. You hear? They're reconstructing. I have enough money for the two of us for the rest of our lives.

AGNES: I'd rather work. I'm leaving you.

CHARACTER: Oh!

AGNES: I'll miss you, though. I've given you almost three years of my youth. Will you miss me? Will you be a little bit sorry at least?

The CHARACTER shakes his head yes.

It hurts me to hurt you.

CHARACTER: I dreamed I was walking on a rope bridge over a ravine.

He goes to his armchair and sits down. She makes ready to leave. She goes out, comes back with a suitcase, packs it, closes it.

AGNES: There are songs out there, there's light. (*She exits again and comes back a few times with items for her suitcases.*) You could help me close my suitcases. You look like you've got the whole world on your back. You're afraid to move, you're scared someone will grab you up. Don't bother closing your eyes, that won't help. It only makes you feel dizzier. Look, you have two extremes: either you jump around nervously or you stay in your armchair and not move at all.

CHARACTER: Because everything is shaky.

She exits again and returns with more things and another suitcase.

AGNES: I had a hard time deciding, you know. I would've stayed with you but you're too . . . you're too much like you are. And besides, I want to get back to work. I want to go out, I want to get married and have children. Help me with the suitcases; don't be such a stump!

She works at her suitcases and he makes a ridiculous attempt at helping her by bringing her a piece of lingerie, a handkerchief, or a piece of paper.
The CONCIERGE *enters. She looks older, and little by little, with each entrance, she gets older and older.*

CONCIERGE: I called for a taxi. He's downstairs.

AGNES (*to* CONCIERGE): I thought that I'd cure him of his sickness.

CONCIERGE (*to the* CHARACTER): Well, look what you've brought upon yourself.

AGNES (*to the* CHARACTER): Help me carry my suitcases down at least, will you?

CONCIERGE: You've got three, I'll take one.

The CONCIERGE *picks up the largest one and disappears with it. The* CHARACTER *takes a suitcase and exits with it.*

AGNES (*alone stage center, looks around her, the suitcase at her feet*): It's been four years after all. It was interesting, he's an interesting man. I'll remember him.

The CHARACTER *enters. He makes an attempt to pick up the last suitcase.*

Don't bother, I'll manage. Come and give me a kiss good-bye, at least. Come on, don't be shy.

He kisses her on her forehead lightly.

Don't forget me, okay? I mean, don't forget me right away. I left you my photo. You're not too sad, are you? It's life. I'll write you. I'll send you postcards of beautiful places.

She takes the last suitcase and exits. The CHARACTER *remains standing, stage center. He looks a little lost, his arms hang down. His expression changes and becomes dull, indifferent. He goes to his armchair and sits down. The* CONCIERGE *enters.*

CONCIERGE: She asked me to bring you these papers and two bottles of brandy. She said she'd think about you. She's already sent a postcard. Look, she says herself: tell him that I'll think of him often. She's in a faraway country in the south. She's with her fiancé. (*She puts the two bottles of brandy next to his armchair. She hands him the newspapers.*) Ever since the war is over, the papers have become interesting again. Look at what's written here: You see a family man murdered his wife and son with an ax, while they slept. A woman shot her husband and his daughter to death. Two lovers committed suicide in a hotel room. The body of a drowned girl, who had mysteriously disappeared, was found in the Seine, floating and puffy. A Frenchman married a Japanese girl and then leaves her for a German girl. The Japanese girl commits hara-kiri. The world will die because there won't be any more oxygen. Astronauts are on the moon and are sending messages down that they're bored. The Vatican comes out for charity among men. Now wars are outlawed. So in one country people play killing games called war. The ASPCA wants us to stop killing baby seals. (*The* CONCIERGE *puts the papers under the* CHARACTER'S *arm.*) There's enough to read for a while. That'll distract you. Now all those everyday happenings have come back into their own. That's the way it is, one drop of blood these days goes a long way. We don't need oceans-full anymore.

She exits. During the course of the next scene, the décor disappears piece by piece. If possible, the furniture should be made to disappear too, except for the chair the CHARACTER *sits in. At the end, he should be alone on stage. The décor should be made to disappear by means of pulleys, flattening of buffets, etc. This should be done as smoothly, noiselessly as possible. In order to mark the passage of time with means other than the* CONCIERGE *visibly getting older with each entrance, we should see morning, sundown and night from the windows, and they should succeed each other faster and faster. At the end there is a new, younger* CONCIERGE . . . *the* CONCIERGE'S *daughter who looks exactly like the* CONCIERGE *did at the beginning. We hear singing outside, walking steps, construction noises. The* CHARACTER *has remained in his armchair reading his paper, drinking brandy, not noticing any of the changes, of course.*

CHARACTER: Who is it?

CONCIERGE (*enters*): Here's your dinner, sir.

She puts down the tray and takes out the one she had put down previously. She'll repeat this action at each entrance.

Yes, yes, she was here! There's still a slipper of hers she forgot, down there under your chair. She also left her umbrella in the umbrella stand.

CHARACTER: Then it was true? There was someone here?

The CONCIERGE *exits. He reads on. Noises outside, décor disappears.* CONCIERGE *returns.*

CONCIERGE: If you want to go out . . . I won't insist. You look so tired. It's age. You retired too young, sir. I have trouble climbing the stairs myself. The elevator doesn't work anymore. I've got rhumatism. They want to build another elevator. Outside, there's singing, marching, building. People aren't amusing anymore. They've gotten into strange habits now, they've always got to be doing something. In the morning, it's gymnastics. They all stop in the middle of everything at the same hour and they do their exercising. That's a decision of the new government. Here are the new papers, I'll take the others.

She exits. She returns.

Here's your food. Well, will you contribute to the construction of the new elevator?

He shakes his head yes. He eats distractedly. She exits. Enters, looking older.

Another mealtime. What a lovely evening. We didn't get permission to build a new elevator. They want to build a new building here instead. We were the last-standing building of the original construction on this block. All around us, new walls are going up. They want to change everything, tear down everything. Rebuild everything. They've got to keep rebuilding if they want to keep demolishing. Then there'll be a new revolution and new destruction. And new reconstruction. And it'll never stop! It'll all start over again. Sleep well, sir. You don't have a blanket left? Here's one.

She exits. The stage becomes almost totally dark. During this blackout, décor may be taken away. Lights up. Stage is emptier. The CONCIERGE *enters, older.*

Here's your breakfast, sir. And the papers. You're sure you wouldn't like a radio or television?

She exits, taking the tray with her as she leaves.

Oh my legs! Those stairs, day in, day out. You sure you wouldn't like to have your meals in a restaurant?

She exits. A long pause. She enters, followed by the PROPRIETOR *of the restaurant, much older. The* CONCIERGE *is now walking with a cane. The* PROPRIETOR *might have one also. The* CHARACTER *should age too, but in a much less obvious manner.*

PROPRIETOR*: Don't you recognize me?

CONCIERGE: I'm bringing you two meals. This gentleman is a friend of yours, he wants to have lunch with you. You know, the restaurant . . . where you used to eat, where you met Agnes?

CHARACTER: Agnes?

PROPRIETOR (*as the* CONCIERGE *exits*): I learned that you were still here. We haven't seen you in so long. I thought you were dead. Do you remember? You used to eat in my place every day. It must be thirty years ago, thirty-five maybe. You're one of the rare survivors among my old customers. So I wanted to see you. My restaurant was half wrecked during the revolution. Now it's been reconstructed. I have a brand-new restaurant and brand-new personnel. A modern place with all the conveniences. There are a lot of young people who come in. I have a discotheque downstairs in the cellar. You remember the cellar? Ah, those were the good old days. I recognize you all right, you haven't changed much. That's because you don't work. You're still rich as ever, eh? You remember, they shot at us through the windows from the outside, they broke everything. And then we shot back at them. Not us, I mean the customers did. Ah, the good old days. You recall how they screamed and yelled and machine-gunned and ran. You remember the

---

* *This scene with the* PROPRIETOR *was omitted in the Parisian production of the play.*

young man who was shot outside on the sidewalk, lying in a pool of blood? Oh was that a laugh . . . the cops took the mother away to the precinct and not the killers. I should have been in charge of the revolution, but I was already too old. How old was I then? Forty? Forty-five? I didn't want any more, I had settled down. Oh boy, oh boy. I had already headed the previous revolution. Once a lifetime, that's enough. Hey, your housekeeper is a good cook. She makes up nice little dishes for you, I see. Oh, there's your faithful brandy bottle, eh? I like good red wine better. White wine too, sometimes. They broke bottles of my good stuff. I replaced them and they broke those. The war's over, but there's still fighting. But I guess that's rare enough. They're much quieter, the young people of today. They sing, they construct, they do their gymnastics on government orders. Every now and then, oh, rarely enough, someone gets out of line and has his head bashed in. They come and pick him up. Repression is pretty well organized for the time being. Brawling is outlawed now. It gets in the way of reconstruction. Troublemakers are antisocial. That means against society these days. Now things're calm. Oh, I miss the good old days. You remember the punch in the nose you got when you tried to defend Yvonne, no, it was Agnes. I want to get my old customers back, those that are still alive, of course. Life goes by so quickly. We all are mortal after all, aren't we?

The light dims.

Well, it really does go by quickly, doesn't it? I've spent the whole afternoon with you. No, I won't stay for dinner. Besides I've got to get back to my restaurant. It was closed for lunch. They're getting ready for dinner now. I've got to see to things. You've got to come and take a look at these young people and new people of today working in my place. Now some of them are twenty and weren't even born during the revolution, there are some who are forty, others who are fifty. They'll be surprised to see you, I've talked to them a lot about you. You'll tell them the story. They haven't heard your side of the resistance, the civil war, fascism, Stalin, DeGaulle, the republic . . . they've got to hear it. They don't know. But are we even sure that we know ourselves? (*He gets up with difficulty, visibly older than before, leaning on his cane. The street is brightly lit now, brighter lamps. They light up the whole apartment. He exits.*) Goodbye.

CHARACTER: Turn off the lights!

The stage goes dark. A few instants of silence, suddenly morning light. The room is emptier still. The CONCIERGE *enters, older, completely hunchbacked now, walking with crutches.*

CONCIERGE: I don't think I'll be able to come up here much longer. Here's your breakfast. And your newspapers.

She exits. AGNES *enters, an old lady.*

AGNES: Hello, dear. I was passing through the city. I found the street by some miracle, everything's so changed. They told me you were still here. Don't you recognize me? We spent four years together. I never forgot you. I thought of you often. I sent you letters. Did you ever get them? I left because you were afraid of me. You remember? It was a morning like this. I've been happy. I'm a widow now. But I've got wonderful memories. I always had a good memory. And besides, who could forget you? You see how things changed. Things move, nothing stays the same. I wanted to see you before it was too late. Do you know who I am?

He remains silent.

Do you know who I am? I had six children, there're only five left. They're all married. They have their own children, they're fifteen in all. Fifteen times a grandmother. What's my name? You don't even know. What's my name, come on now?

CHARACTER: Lucienne.

AGNES: No, no, no.

CHARACTER: Jacqueline.

AGNES: Have I changed that much? Yes, I suppose I have changed.

CHARACTER: Yvonne?

AGNES: No, no, no. I'm Agnes! The punch in the nose? You were all bloody. I cleaned your face and I came to your house. We slipped under the iron shutter. The white flag that you waved outside? Shot through with a bloody bullet.

CHARACTER: Oh, yes, the punch in the nose. Those were the good old days. And the suitcases!

AGNES (*laughing*): You really were clumsy. You couldn't even shut one suitcase for me. I took the train when I left here. It was sunny and I was very sad, very. But I've been happy, I must say. It's the truth. I'm still an optimist. There's the church bell, it's noon already. I was glad I could see you and we had such a good talk. Just like in the old days, eh? I'll have to go, my grandchildren are waiting. They're downstairs in the car. Help me to get up, will you? I can't get out of this chair, help me.

The CHARACTER *doesn't move.* AGNES *gets up by herself anyway.*

I'll kiss you goodbye.

She doesn't kiss him. She exits, hopping like a cripple. The CONCIERGE *comes in, but this time she's young, as she was at the beginning of the play.*

CONCIERGE: Here's your lunch.

CHARACTER: Who are you?

CONCIERGE: Mom can't climb the stairs anymore, she's paralyzed. I'm taking her place.

She exits. The CHARACTER *remains motionless for a few instants. Night falls. The* CONCIERGE *returns.*

CONCIERGE: Here's your dinner. The lady is dead.

CHARACTER: What lady?

CONCIERGE: The lady who came to see you last week, a month ago, your old mistress. She's dead.

CHARACTER: Turn off the lights.

The stage goes dark. Again the lights come up on morning. The CONCIERGE *enters, she's dressed in mourning.*

CONCIERGE: Here's your breakfast. And your papers. Mom is dead. I won't be working for you much longer. I'm going to work with my husband. They still haven't put in an elevator, and besides being a servant doesn't interest me.

She exits, taking the old tray with her. She is much tougher than her mother was. After a few short moments, she returns.

Here are your canned goods. But you might as well know, they're tearing down the house. They've torn down everything else on all sides. They're planning a huge civic square right here.

She exits. She returns after a few moments.

Here's your dinner.

CHARACTER: Thanks. Turn off the lights.

The stage goes dark. After a few moments, the lights come up again. We hear the comings and goings of the CONCIERGE, who mumbles constantly. The pace picks up as the CONCIERGE brings in and takes out trays furiously. As she does, she repeats: Your breakfast, Your papers, Here's your lunch, Your dinner, in rapid succession. This is punctuated by the CHARACTER's Turn out the lights after each dinner. So that the audience does not think that the blackouts indicate the end of the play, perhaps there should be some light remaining on stage, and we can see the silhouettes of the CHARACTER and the CONCIERGE. We can see the furniture disappearing with each dimout also.

During the obscurity, the noises coming from outside

pick up, and we hear laughter, singing, street sounds, construction noises, see sharp lights indicating welding machines used in the construction of the buildings going up all around. Between the comings and goings of the CONCIERGE *and during the blackouts, several characters will act out rapid pieces of action. The dead return to talk to the* CHARACTER, *but they should not have the appearance of ghosts.*

MOTHER OF CHARACTER: I told you, my son, I told you to work hard. I told you that, ever since you were a little boy. I would've liked you to have another kind of life. Ah, if only you had done well in school as I told you to, you could have become an army captain with a beautiful uniform and decoration, lots of decorations. I suffered so much for you. I loved you so much. My poor little boy, poor little boy.

She disappears.

LUCIENNE: My love, I've been dead so long, but I've never forgotten you. I never forgave myself for leaving you for Pierre. I never loved him. It was you I loved. I suffered so much for you. I loved you so much, so much.

She disappears.

CHARACTER'S SCHOOL TEACHER: I was your teacher at school. You were a good-for-nothing. You were a rotten student. But I would've so much loved to do something for you, be proud of you. You caused me a lot of pain because I was very fond of you, very fond.

AGNES' DAUGHTER: I'm Agnes' daughter, my name is Agnes, like my mother. She died two years ago. She came to see you before she died. She made me promise I'd come to see you. My mother loved you very much, she adored you.

She exits. During these monologues, the CHARACTER *remains seated and motionless and expressionless.*

JACQUES DUPONT'S SON: I'm Jacques Dupont's son. Do you recognize me? I look like my father. My father was very fond of you, you know. He was sad after you left the company. He always hoped you'd go back and visit him once. You promised to go back and have a drink with him. He was very fond of you, very fond.

He exits.

YOUNG MAN, SON OF LOVER OF WOMAN WITH DOG: I'm the son of the young man who ran off with the lady with the dog, forty years ago. My father liked you a lot. So did the lady. You never went to tea at her house. She was very sorry about that, because she liked you very much. You have no idea how much she liked you.

He exits.

SON OF REVOLUTIONARY WHO PUNCHED CHARACTER IN NOSE: I'm the son of the revolutionary who punched you in the nose. My father asked me to come to see you to tell you how sorry he was about that. He liked you, had nothing personal against you. He liked you a lot.

He exits. During these speeches the CHARACTER *doesn't react but continues to drink brandy. Two other men enter.*

TWO MEN: We like you a lot.

They exit. A woman enters.

WOMAN: Oh, kind sir, I loved you in secret for so long. I never dared tell you. We could never have been happy. I never had the courage to tell you how much I loved you from a distance.

She exits. All the people who came forward now reappear together and stand in different corners of the stage. They extend their arms toward the CHARACTER.

ALL: We loved you!

CHARACTER: You rats! Get the hell out of here!

The CHARACTER *rises and throws the brandy bottle at them and then a can of food. They disperse and disappear.*

Get the hell out! Lights! Turn on the lights!

The morning light brightens the stage. We hear no noises from the outside. The walls have disappeared, the stage is brightened by brilliant light. As furniture, only the armchair remains, stage center.

Housekeeper! My breakfast! I want my breakfast. Housekeeper?

He runs across the stage, looking right and left.

My breakfast! I want my breakfast at once!

He keeps running and looks for the CONCIERGE *to enter.*

What's going on? There's no one around! Hey? Anybody there?

He runs over to the brandy bottle, picks it up, and hurls it.

I'm going to die of hunger. I'll die of thirst too.

He looks all around him at the empty space basking in the strange illumination.

What's the meaning of all this? Housekeeper? All right! It's no use, there's nobody here. I don't understand what's going on and there's no point trying. No one could understand. And yet somehow I'm not surprised. In fact it's surprising that I'm not surprised. Very surprising.

We see a huge, leafy tree come forward from the illumination upstage. It's in full bloom of both leaf and flower. Some fall, and the CHARACTER *bends down to pick them up. He looks at them curiously, looks left and right.*

He goes over and sits in his armchair, remains quiet a moment, then starts to laugh quietly. The laughter grows and becomes uproarious. Then he gets up, still laughing, walking, holding his belly, becoming convulsive. He finally looks up toward heaven and shakes his finger vigorously.

Ah, you rascal . . . rascal!

He continues to laugh hysterically.

Oh, that's a good one. That's incredible. I should have realized it a long time ago. What a joke! It's fantastic! What a gag! What a huge, overdone gag! And I worried and suffered, and . . .

Turns toward upstage.

What a joke!

Toward stage right.

Ha, ha, ha, what a good, bad joke!

Toward stage left.

What a long, drawn out, overrated, bad joke, ha, ha, ha.

Still laughing, toward the audience.

What a joke, my friends. Ha, ha, ha . . . oh, the laugh's on us, ha, ha, who could have thought up one like this? Ha, ha, what a mess, ha, ha, ha, ha. What a hell of a mess! Ha, ha, ha.